"The Cosmic Conflict: War of The Gods"

Author: Kenneth Ocasio

Published by Book Writer Corner

ISBN: 978-1-960815-80-4

DEDICATED

To my son, Jacob,

For every question you posed, every conversation we delved into, every text exchanged, and each spirited argument that pushed the boundaries of my understanding – thank you. It is because of you that I embarked on this journey of relentless research and deep introspection. You ignited the flame of curiosity and challenged me to seek, to know, and to grow. This book is not just a testament to my journey but to ours.

With endless gratitude and love,
Dad.

Contents

ACKNOWLEDGMENTS

Writing a book is seldom a solitary journey, and this work is a testament to the collective effort of a community that believed in its vision and significance.

To those who generously contributed financially, your support was not just monetary but an investment in the propagation of knowledge and understanding. It allowed this idea to take shape, grow, and finally come to fruition. Your faith in this endeavor was the bedrock upon which it was built.

To the countless souls who upheld this project in prayer, I am deeply humbled. It's said that where words fail, prayers speak, and I felt every whisper of hope, every plea for wisdom, and every invocation for clarity. The spiritual fortification provided by your intercessions was invaluable, and it often served as the guiding light during the challenging phases of this project.

And to those who offered words of encouragement, advice, and constructive critique – thank you for being the wind beneath my wings. Every message, call, and conversation was a reminder that this work mattered, not just to me, but to many. Your belief in me, especially during moments of doubt, was the catalyst that propelled me forward.

To each and every one of you – thank you for being part of this journey. This book, while penned by one, is the embodiment of the love, support, and faith of many.

Warmly,
Kenneth Ocasio
thecosmicconflict.com

Introduction: Unraveling the Enigma of Cosmic Conflict

Two decades ago, my life was interjected by a fleeting curiosity—a seemingly innocuous thought about the cosmos and our place within it. At that time, it seemed more of an interesting divergence than a lifelong pursuit. Little did I know; that this spark of intrigue would mold the course of my intellectual and spiritual journey.

The year 2020 brought with it unparalleled challenges. As the world hunkered down, grappling with the strangeness and uncertainty ushered in by a global pandemic, a unique opportunity arose. The imposed solitude of the COVID-19 shutdown brought with it the gift of introspection, the quiet moments that life's busyness often robs from us.

I found myself returning to that old spark, the nagging question about the cosmos that had once captured my imagination. I delved into scriptures anew, seeking out age-old wisdom with a fresh perspective. The biblical texts, which I thought I knew, began to unfold in unexpected ways, revealing nuances and depths I'd previously missed.

My explorations took me beyond personal study. Conversations with rabbis opened my eyes to millennia of teachings and interpretations, adding layers of depth to my understanding. Their insights, often divergent from my own beliefs, challenged and enriched my perspective, reminding me of the vast expanse of human spiritual experience.

Yet, amidst all these scholarly dialogues, it was the earnest conversations with my son that became the cornerstone of this journey. Our passionate debates, our shared wonder, and our moments of awe deepened our bond and enriched the narrative of this book. His youthful perspective, combined with his zeal for discovery, often led our discussions down paths I hadn't anticipated, pushing the boundaries of my own understanding.

This journey has been as humbling as it has been enlightening. Every revelation illuminated how little we truly know in the grand scheme of things. Yet, in recognizing our own limitations, we open ourselves to the boundless mysteries of the divine, waiting to be explored.

As this book reaches its conclusion, my journey doesn't. I feel a reinvigorated commitment to delve deeper into scripture, engage more meaningfully with fellow believers, and reach out with compassion to those ensnared by dark forces. With the armor of God shielding me and His word guiding me, I am poised to play my part in this cosmic drama, hoping to shine His light in every dark corner and reclaim souls for the Kingdom of Heaven.

To all who have ventured with me through these pages, I pray that you, too, will be inspired to understand your pivotal role in this great saga. May you be equipped and emboldened to spread the love and truth of God, ensuring that His kingdom thrives amidst the chaos and that every lost soul finds its way home.

May we remain steadfast, and may our journeys, individual and collective, always reflect His grace and wisdom.

Chapter 1

The Origin of the Cosmic Conflict

"In the beginning..." (Genesis 1:1)

The cosmic conflict is more than just a fanciful tale spun to explain earthly strife. To fully grasp the intricacies of this ancient battle, one must peer beyond the veil of the material and into the spiritual realm, where events of cosmic significance were set in motion long before humankind took its first steps.

We can glean invaluable insight into the celestial conflict by examining the Old Testament and its associated cultures. Utilizing biblical literature, ancient Near Eastern manuscripts, and theological scholarship, we can see a comprehensive perspective of a realm seldom observed by the general populace - a realm replete with divine entities and formidable energies.

The early chapters of the Book of Genesis set the stage. The phrase "sons of God" (*bene Elohim in Hebrew*) appears in several instances. *In Genesis 6:1-4*, these entities are depicted as marrying the "daughters of men," producing a line of hybrid giants called the Nephilim. It's evident that the "sons of God" were not humans, but rather divine or angelic beings, a notion reinforced by parallel passages in Job (*1:6; 2:1; 38:7*). This intermingling represents not just a physical encroachment but also a deliberate attempt by these beings to derail God's plans for humanity. The Flood narrative can be perceived not just as a judgment on human wickedness but also on these illicit unions and their offspring.

Delving deeper into the Old Testament, I would like to draw our attention to *Psalm 82*, where God presides over an assembly of gods, passing judgment on them for their corrupt rulership over the nations. The prophet Daniel, too, speaks of divine beings— 'princes' — assigned to various countries, with Michael identified as the protector of Israel (*Daniel 10:13, 20-21*).

These accounts suggest that after the events of Babel, the nations were handed over to lesser divine beings who were supposed to govern justly, in alignment with Yahweh's decrees. However, they became corrupt, leading the nations astray. The fallout from this cosmic rebellion is profound; the gods set themselves up as objects of worship, directly opposing Yahweh and leading humanity down paths of idolatry.

The Apostle Paul, too, echoed the understanding of this spiritual battle. In his letter to the Ephesians, he reminds believers that their battle is not against flesh and blood but "against the rulers, against the authorities, against the cosmic powers over this present darkness, against the spiritual forces of evil in the heavenly places" (*Ephesians 6:12*). The New Testament thus acknowledges an ongoing cosmic struggle, rooted in the actions and decisions of divine beings who have rebelled against their Creator.

Yet, why would such powerful entities rebel against an omnipotent God? Biblical narratives and ancient Near Eastern texts suggest a mix of pride, desire for autonomy, and, at times, direct opposition to God's plans, especially concerning humanity. Despite their power, these beings were created and thus susceptible to the same pitfalls of ambition and pride that often plague society.

The Book of Revelation provides a climax to this celestial drama. The dragon (interpreted as Satan or the Devil) and his angels wage war against Michael and his angels, resulting in the dragon being cast out of heaven *(Revelation 12:7-9)*. This expulsion is not just a defeat for these rebellious entities; it signals the eventual restoration of God's order in both the celestial and terrestrial realms.

What does this mean for humanity? Firstly, it's crucial to recognize that we knowingly or unknowingly participate in this cosmic drama. Our decisions, allegiances, and actions have implications that ripple through the spiritual realm. Secondly, God's ultimate intent is restoring all things, a cosmos where justice, peace, and righteousness reign. The biblical narrative assures us that despite the formidable powers opposing God, His sovereignty remains unchallenged.

The cosmic conflict is neither a mere backdrop nor a theological abstraction. It is deeply rooted in the spiritual dynamics that influence our world. By recognizing and understanding this, we can navigate our lives with a clearer sense of purpose rooted in the knowledge of God's ultimate victory.

The realm that is not visible to the naked eye is not a mere fabrication of folklore or fable. Instead, it is the factual existence that the Bible has expounded upon since its inception. This realm serves as the backdrop for the entirety of the narrative. And as we engage with this story, we find our place within this grand, divine narrative, ultimately pointing us toward hope, redemption, and restoration.

Echoes of the Celestial: Humanity's Dance with the Cosmic Conflict

Throughout human history, the undercurrent of the cosmic conflict has rippled through our stories, societies, and daily spiritual journeys. Far from being a distant, nebulous warfare, this celestial struggle casts its shadow and light upon every aspect of our existence. Let's journey through the annals of time and personal experiences to grasp the profound influence of this unseen realm.

The annals of human history are replete with accounts of the celestial realm, divine interventions, and enigmatic encounters. These narratives have exerted a profound influence on the development of civilizations, served as a source of inspiration for artistic masterpieces, and engendered philosophical debates that have persisted for millennia. Yet, when viewed through the prism of the cosmic struggle, these echoes of the celestial assume a profound significance. Humanity's engagement with these divine phenomena, from ancient folklore to contemporary reports of unidentified flying objects, symbolizes a larger engagement with the cosmic spiritual warfare that undergirds the fabric of reality.

Since civilization's dawn, societies have been molded by their spiritual beliefs. Myths, legends, and religious narratives from various cultures often tell of battles between gods, heroes, and monsters, hinting at a greater cosmic history. These tales, seen through the lens of the biblical cosmic conflict, are not just fantasies but echoes of a deeper reality. While cultural details differ, the underlying theme is consistent: a battle between good and evil, order and chaos.

Human history itself can be perceived as a series of confrontations influenced by this spiritual warfare. Empires have risen and fallen, often with leaders claiming divine favor or mandate. Wars have been waged in the name of gods or against perceived heresies. Behind the physical, political, and territorial disputes, cosmic forces have been at play, vying for influence over human hearts and nations.

Society, too, reflects this celestial struggle. Injustice, oppression, and the various ills we witness can be traced back to the corrupt rulership of those rebellious spiritual entities mentioned in *Psalm 82*. Just as they failed in their divine mandates, societies under their influence veer away from justice, mercy, and righteousness.

Yet, it's not just on the macro scale of nations and cultures that we see the effects of the cosmic conflict. Its most profound impact is on the micro-scale, within the hearts and minds of individuals. Regardless of creed or background, every human engages in a daily spiritual battle, often manifesting as struggles with temptation, doubt, purpose, and identity.

Paul's letters are illuminating in this regard. He paints the picture of the believer as a soldier, donning spiritual armor to withstand the schemes of the devil (*Ephesians 6:11-17*). The enemy's fiery darts represent doubts, fears, and temptations aimed to divert believers from their spiritual path. Yet, these battles aren't just for the pious. Everyone, irrespective of their religious stance, grapples with inner conflicts that resonate with the broader cosmic war.

Consider the universal human experience of grappling with inner demons—addictions, insecurities, or despair. Are these not reflections of the more significant spiritual battle, where forces beyond our comprehension attempt to sway our paths? Every act of kindness or cruelty, every decision to uphold integrity or succumb to corruption, every moment of hope or despair becomes a battleground.

Yet, within this daunting framework, there's profound hope. If human history and personal experiences are influenced by cosmic conflict, then they are also under the purview of divine redemption. Moments of grace, acts of selfless love, and societal reforms are a testament to the working of a benevolent power, tirelessly laboring to restore creation.

Stories of personal transformation, where individuals overcome their deepest fears and vices, can be perceived as victories in the spiritual realm. Whenever a person chooses love over hate, service over selfishness, or hope over despair, it's a testament to the resilience of the human spirit and, perhaps, the influence of divine powers championing our cause.

Furthermore, the cosmic narrative offers purpose and direction during these battles. Understanding that our struggles are part of a larger story provides context and meaning. It reminds us that we're not alone in our fights and that there's a greater power available to guide, protect, and uplift.

The cosmic conflict is not a remote tale; rather, it is intricately intertwined with the very essence of human history, society, and individual experiences. Although it presents obstacles, enticements, and struggles, it also provides a storyline of optimism, salvation, and divine intervention. Recognizing its influence helps us navigate life with a deeper sense of purpose, knowing that our choices echo in eternity and contribute to a grand, unfolding story of restoration.

The Cosmic Conflict in Christian Theology: The Heartbeat of Redemption

As it reverberates through the corridors of time, the cosmic conflict has always been of paramount significance in Christian theology. Its narrative not only unveils the metaphysical backdrop against which the entire biblical drama unfolds, but it also offers profound insights into God's character, human purpose, and the destiny of creation.

At its core, Christian theology revolves around the person and work of Jesus Christ. But to comprehend the profundity of Christ's incarnation, crucifixion, and resurrection, one must first grasp the overarching cosmic narrative that necessitated such a divine intervention. We must understand:

1. *The Nature and Character of God:*

The cosmic conflict illuminates God's character in several pivotal ways. First, it underscores His respect for free will. The very existence of a celestial rebellion attests to God's allowance for genuine freedom among His created beings. He does not coerce loyalty or impose robotic allegiance. This freedom, while leading to rebellion in some entities, is essential for genuine love and relationships.

Secondly, God's response to the rebellion—predicated on redemption rather than mere obliteration—underscores His grace, mercy, and commitment to restoration. The lengths He goes to in the person of Jesus Christ to reconcile creation to Himself is a powerful testament to His unyielding love.

The sprawling narrative of the cosmic conflict, encompassing the timeless struggle of good versus evil, unfurls a majestic backdrop against which the nature and character of God are magnified. As the shadows cast by the forces of darkness seek to diminish the luminance of the Divine, both Scripture and personal encounters with God paint an image that beams with enduring love, unerring justice, and boundless sovereignty.

Alongside love, the pillars of justice and righteousness form the foundation upon which God's throne is erected, as articulated in Psalm 89:14, "Righteousness and justice are the foundation of your throne; love and faithfulness go before you." Central to the cosmic dispute, these attributes often find themselves in the crosshairs of doubt and critique. But as the overarching narrative unfolds, God's pristine justice is progressively revealed. The cross becomes the epitome of this revelatory journey, a juncture where divine love and justice intersect seamlessly. Here, sin is judiciously addressed, not overlooked, and the gift of salvation is magnanimously extended, epitomizing a God who is just and simultaneously a redeemer.

The cosmic narrative also presents a fascinating dance between the vastness of God's sovereignty and the delicate exercise of human free will. In His boundless power, God could effortlessly suppress any form of rebellion. Yet, He bestows free will, even when it beckons choices that defy His divine blueprint. This isn't a manifestation of divine vulnerability but an eloquent testament to God's longing for authentic love and worship. Despite the ebb and flow of chaos, God's overarching sovereignty ensures the final word always rests with Him.

In this grand theater of cosmic conflict, God's dual nature of being transcendent and immanent shines forth. His transcendence is a comforting reminder of His supreme vantage point from which He guides the grand narrative to its preordained climax. Concurrently, His immanence, crystallized in the incarnation of Christ, reflects a God willing to dive deep into the trenches to resonate with his creation's joys, sorrows, and aspirations.

The unfolding timeline of the cosmic drama prompts many to ponder the enduring existence of evil in a realm crafted by a loving Creator. Here, God's profound patience emerges as the answer. As *2 Peter 3:9* articulates, God's patience stems not from a place of indecision but from a profound longing to extend the olive branch of salvation to the broadest spectrum of souls.

Throughout this tumultuous journey, God's communicative essence ensures humanity is never left to wander in darkness. From the prophetic utterances of old to the life and teachings of Jesus, from the apocalyptic visions etched in Revelation to the myriad testimonies echoing today, God's voice consistently pierces the cacophony, offering guidance, solace, and hope.

In summation, as the cosmic conflict rages on, the radiant character of God stands tall, impervious to the enemy's constant attempts at defamation. Grasping the depths of His love, justice, sovereignty, patience, and communicative essence equips souls to find solace and actively partake in this grand celestial battle, aligning with the eternal King of the cosmos.

2. The Plight of Humanity:

Understanding the cosmic conflict helps us grasp the gravity of human sin and its consequences. Humanity's fall wasn't an isolated incident but a crucial event in a grander celestial drama. Sin isn't merely a list of wrongdoings; it's allegiance to forces opposing God. The weight of sin, thus, carries cosmic implications.

Given the high stakes, the question of allegiance becomes paramount. Allegiance to God is not a mere religious or ritualistic act; it's a conscious alignment with the ultimate force of love, justice, and righteousness in the universe. This allegiance fortifies the human spirit against deception, provides clarity amidst chaos, and ensures an eternal place within God's kingdom.

When we openly profess our allegiance to God, it's not just a mere declaration; it's an active engagement with a deep wellspring of divine might and safeguarding. This commitment provides access to resources that far exceed human comprehension or capabilities. The book of Ephesians, in its sixth chapter, vividly paints a picture of the "armor of God." It's not a physical set of armor but a collection of spiritual assets and protective measures that God offers to those who have chosen to align their hearts and lives with Him. Each piece, from the belt of truth to the shield of faith, serves a distinct and crucial purpose. They are designed to defend against the devil's subtle deceptions and evil intents and fortify believers, enabling them to withstand the intense and often unseen battles that rage in the spiritual realm. By donning this divine armor, believers are equipped to survive these confrontations and emerge victorious, standing resolute and unyielding in their faith even when faced with the most formidable adversarial forces.

Moreover, allegiance to God transcends a simplistic give-and-take equation. It's much more than a transactional relationship, akin to how one might interact with a vending machine, inserting obedience and expecting blessings in return. Instead, it's a profound, transformative journey that has the power to reshape the very core of our being. As we draw nearer to God, our character undergoes a metamorphosis, gradually mirroring the divine attributes of love, compassion, and righteousness. Our will, often fragmented by worldly desires and distractions, begins to synchronize harmoniously with the intentions of our Creator. This alignment infuses our existence with a profound sense of purpose and meaning, grounding us in a reality beyond earthly life's transient nature. By actively choosing God, we aren't merely selecting an affiliation in a grand cosmic battle between good and evil. We wholeheartedly embrace a path that promises spiritual maturation and deep fulfillment on Earth and paves the way to a blissful eternity in communion with God.

3. *The Mission of Christ:*

The Incarnation becomes even more profound within the context of this conflict. Jesus enters a world held hostage by principalities and powers to defeat them and reclaim what was lost. His crucifixion is the pivotal moment where the forces of darkness are seemingly victorious. Still, it is precisely in this moment of apparent defeat that Christ triumphs over them (And having disarmed the powers and authorities, he made a public spectacle of them, triumphing over them by the cross. *Colossians 2:15*).

The Resurrection isn't just a demonstration of divine power; it's the inaugural event signaling the eventual end of the cosmic conflict, ensuring hope and restoration for creation. It's the promise that victory is assured though the battle rages now.

Christ's involvement in the vast cosmic conflict extended far beyond His triumphant resurrection. After rising from the dead, He didn't merely fade into the annals of history. Instead, He ascended to the heavens, taking on the profoundly significant role of our High Priest. From this exalted position, He passionately intercedes for humanity, standing as a mediator between us and the Father. Every prayer, every cry of anguish, every plea for forgiveness finds its way to Him, and He presents them before God, cloaked in His righteousness.

Moreover, as our divine guide, Christ plays an instrumental role in directing our spiritual paths. His teachings, life, and ever-present Spirit steer us toward deeper understandings, growth, and communion with the Divine. In His infinite love, He is also meticulously preparing a dwelling for those He has redeemed—a place free from sorrow, pain, and the ravages of time.

His promise to return to Earth is not a mere footnote in scripture but a monumental event that marks the impending climax of the cosmic narrative. This return won't be as a sacrificial lamb but as a conquering king, heralding the final dissolution of evil and the restoration of creation to its initial, untarnished glory. Christ emerges as the consistent centerpiece throughout the countless millennia of this vast heavenly battle. He stands as the beacon of hope, radiating light in the darkest corners of the universe. He embodies unwavering love and the unshakable guarantee of triumph for all who choose to align with His righteous cause.

4. *The Role of the Church:*

The church is not merely an institution for communal worship. Within the cosmic conflict narrative, it is the assembly of those aligned with God's kingdom against the forces of darkness. Every act of evangelism, discipleship, and service becomes a means of advancing God's kingdom, pushing back against the spiritual forces opposing it. In the overarching narrative of the cosmic conflict, the church isn't a mere spectator. It's an active participant, a frontline warrior, and a guiding star. As darkness attempts to shroud the world, the church, fueled by the Holy Spirit, shines brighter, illuminating the path for countless souls, guiding them toward eternal redemption and the triumphant culmination of the age-old battle between good and evil.

In the grand tapestry of the cosmic conflict, the church occupies a role of profound significance. Instituted as the body of Christ on Earth, the church stands as both a beacon of light amidst the prevailing darkness and a vanguard in ongoing spiritual warfare. Entrusted with the Gospel message, the church's mission is to guide its members in understanding and embracing their divine identity and purpose and to shine the light of Christ's redemptive love to the world, drawing souls towards salvation. When unified and fortified by the Holy Spirit, the church becomes an indomitable force against the enemy's wiles. Its worship, teachings, and acts of service are not just expressions of faith but are powerful tools in pushing back against the tide of deception and spiritual decay.

As the vast cosmic conflict accelerates towards its foretold climax, a time prophesied to end this age-old struggle between good and evil, the church emerges as an institution of paramount importance. It stands as a bulwark of truth in an era rife with deception, ensuring that the pure, undiluted message of the Gospel continues to shine brightly amidst the shadows of falsehood. The church also takes on the mantle of a spiritual nurturer, providing a haven where faith is cultivated, strengthened, and refined. This faith becomes an anchor for believers, helping them navigate the turbulent waters of doubt and uncertainty. Furthermore, the church acts as a rallying point, mobilizing its members for the spiritual skirmishes and battles that lie ahead. It equips them with the knowledge, tools, and conviction to confront and resist the dark forces that seek to destabilize and destroy. In the grand tapestry of God's redemptive plan, the church is not merely a passive observer but an active participant, making it an essential instrument in God's overarching mission to reclaim the lost and restore the entirety of His creation to its intended glory.

5. *Eschatological Implications:*

The overarching narrative of the cosmic conflict profoundly influences and molds Christian eschatology, painting a vivid backdrop against which the end times are understood. The Book of Revelation, with its intricate tapestry of symbolism and prophetic imagery, offers readers a glimpse into the crescendo of this celestial battle. While at times cryptic, its pages herald the imminent downfall of Satan, signaling the end of his reign of deception and malice. Beyond this defeat, Revelation speaks of the rejuvenation of heaven and earth, sweeping away the scars of sin and replacing them with the pristine beauty of God's original design. It also heralds the rise of God's eternal kingdom, where righteousness prevails, and sorrow is no more.

However, the eschatological vision isn't solely focused on broad cosmic events. It holds out a profoundly personal hope for every believer. Beyond the assurance of individual salvation, it promises them a front-row seat in the triumphant finale of this universe-spanning tale. They are not mere spectators but active participants in the victorious climax of the cosmic saga.

In this vast narrative, the church emerges with a pivotal mission. Its foremost duty is to ready both its congregation and the world at large for the impending return of Christ. Through its doctrinal teachings, the passionate enthusiasm of its worship, and its unwavering commitment to outreach, the church breathes life into the hope of the Second Coming. This ensures that, even as the world hurtles towards uncertain times, believers remain spiritually vigilant, their hearts aflame with anticipation and their spirits prepared to welcome their returning Savior.

Eschatology, the study of the ultimate destiny of humanity and the universe, offers profound insights into the final chapters of the cosmic conflict. As the narrative unfolds, eschatological events serve as both warnings and affirmations of the impending climax of the age-old battle between good and evil. Prophecies, as depicted in biblical texts like Daniel and Revelation, paint vivid images of tumultuous times, revealing the intensification of the spiritual war and God's ultimate sovereignty. These prophetic landscapes are replete with signs, wonders, and divine interventions, all pointing towards a denouement wherein evil's reign is finally quieted, and righteousness is established eternally. Eschatological implications emphasize the transient nature of the present world's struggles and reinforce the hope of a new creation free from the scars of conflict. They serve as a clarion call for believers to remain vigilant, faithful, and aligned with God's purpose, as the culmination of the cosmic conflict promises not just an end to the battle but the dawn of an everlasting era of peace and divine communion.

6. *Personal Sanctification:*

At the heart of our spiritual journeys lies the broader narrative of the cosmic conflict, which offers a deeper perspective into our trials and tribulations. This overarching battle between good and evil serves as a lens through which we can view and understand our spiritual struggles. When we embark on the path of sanctification, our aim isn't solely self-betterment or mere moral improvement. Instead, it's an intentional journey of aligning ourselves more closely with the character of Christ and, by extension, actively positioning ourselves on God's side in this grand celestial confrontation.

Sanctification, thus, becomes more than just an internal transformation. It's a powerful declaration of allegiance, showcasing our loyalties in the cosmic conflict. Each time we overcome temptation, each instance where we choose righteousness over sin, we aren't just marking a personal achievement. No matter how seemingly small, these victories echo through the broader spiritual realm. Every act of obedience and step taken in faith fortifies our relationship with God and adds strength to the collective force of righteousness in the universe.

Essentially, our spiritual milestones are intertwined with the larger narrative of good versus evil. With each victory, with each act of love, kindness, and obedience, we grow as individuals and play a crucial role in advancing the cause of light in the overarching story of the cosmic conflict.

The cosmic conflict isn't a mere side story or an incidental theme in the annals of Christian theology. Instead, it stands as the expansive backdrop, the vast stage upon which the enthralling drama of redemption and salvation unfolds. Every biblical narrative, from the fall of the rebellious one to the redemptive work of Christ, finds its place within this grand cosmic theater. It serves as the framework that binds together disparate tales of prophets, kings, and apostles, revealing a cohesive and divine storyline that spans millennia.

For believers, recognizing and understanding the prominence of this cosmic battle provides more than just historical or theological knowledge. It offers a profound depth to their faith, connecting their spiritual experiences to a larger, divine narrative. Every prayer, every act of faith, and every victory over sin isn't just a personal triumph but becomes part of this majestic tapestry of God's grand plan.

Furthermore, seeing one's spiritual journey against the backdrop of this immense conflict bestows upon it a profound sense of purpose and gravitas. It reminds believers that they are not merely passive observers but active participants in a battle of eternal significance. This realization can inspire greater commitment, passion, and urgency in their walk with God, motivating them to live intentionally, aligning their lives with the divine mission, and playing their part in the ultimate victory of good over evil.

It prompts introspection: How should we live if our choices and actions have cosmic ramifications? The answer finds its root in aligning with God's purposes, participating in His redemptive plan, and anchoring hope in the promised culmination of this epic narrative – the complete and final restoration of all things in Christ.

Personal sanctification within the framework of the cosmic conflict is the transformative journey of aligning one's spirit, soul, and body with God's divine will and purpose. As the larger celestial battle between good and evil rages on, every individual is engaged in a microcosmic struggle, navigating the tumultuous waters of temptation, sin, and self. Sanctification becomes a vital component of this personal struggle, anchoring the believer in the truth and holiness of God amidst the deceptive snares of the enemy. It is not merely an external act of piety but an inward metamorphosis, where the Holy Spirit refines and purifies the heart, instilling virtues that reflect Christ's character. This ongoing process not only fortifies the believer against the onslaughts of the enemy in the cosmic conflict but also empowers them to be beacons of light, showcasing the transformative power of God's love and grace to a world trapped in darkness.

As we conclude our exploration of the cosmic conflict, it becomes evident that this grand celestial struggle between good and evil is far more than just a backdrop to our existence; it permeates every facet of our spiritual journey. The battle rages from the broad strokes of cosmic events to the intimate details of personal sanctification, calling each of us to take a stand, understand our place, and align with the divine. Yet, to grasp the full depth of this narrative, we must delve deeper into the heavenly realms, into the very councils of the divine. In our next chapter, "The Divine Council," we will venture into the inner sanctums of the heavenly court, revealing a complex interplay of divine and semi-divine beings and shedding light on God's grand design in orchestrating the affairs of the cosmos. This journey will provide invaluable insights into the council's role, its members, and its influence on humanity's destiny in the unfolding cosmic drama.

Chapter 2

The Divine Council and Spiritual Warfare: Navigating the Cosmic Assembly

God has taken his place in the divine council; in the midst of the gods he holds judgment (Psalm 82:1)

Delving into the realm of spiritual warfare demands more than a cursory glance at visible events; it requires a deep dive into the unseen structures that form the framework of the celestial realms. At the heart of this structure lies the Divine Council, a heavenly assembly that stands as a testament to God's organized approach to cosmic governance. Echoes of this council can be discerned throughout biblical texts, from the Psalms to the prophetic declarations, offering glimpses into the intricacies of divine administration. Unlike Earth's rudimentary and often flawed governance systems, the Divine Council operates with divine precision and purpose. Within its chambers, a host of celestial beings, ranging from archangels to cherubim, gather to deliberate, receive mandates, and participate in the execution of divine decrees. While distinct in their roles and functions, these beings are united under the unwavering and supreme authority of Yahweh, the Creator and Sustainer of all. In this celestial context, many of the spiritual decisions affecting humanity and the cosmos at large are made, setting the stage for the broader narrative of spiritual warfare that unfolds throughout history.

The Divine Council: An Overview

The biblical texts are replete with instances that pull back the veil, offering us glimpses into the intricate framework of the heavenly realm. This isn't merely a vague, nebulous space but a structured, organized assembly, reflecting a divine order that mirrors the precision and purposefulness of its Creator. The existence of this assembly isn't a compromise on monotheism, nor does it dilute the uniqueness of Yahweh's divine supremacy. Instead, it underscores God's penchant for order, his wisdom in delegation, and his intrinsic nature that leans toward relationships and community.

Various divine beings populate this celestial council, each having specific roles and tasks. They are often referenced in scriptures as the "sons of God" or the "host of heaven," these beings are not mere apparitions but entities with agency and purpose. They are distinct, each bringing a unique facet to the workings of the divine council, yet all operate under the overarching sovereignty of Yahweh.

Psalm 82, often seen as a brief yet profound scripture, opens the curtain to an awe-inspiring celestial council. The scene it paints is rich and evocative: God, also called El in some contexts, stands poised and sovereign during a divine assembly, surrounded by other godly beings or entities. This setting is not meant to elevate these entities to the same status as the Supreme God but offers a structured perspective of the divine hierarchy.

What unfolds in this Psalm is not a contest of power or a challenge to God's supremacy. Instead, it's a solemn courtroom scene, with God taking on the role of the righteous judge. These other gods or divine beings, who might be seen as representatives or stewards of different nations or aspects of creation, are held accountable for their actions or, in some cases, inactions. God questions them, particularly on issues of justice, fairness, and the care of the vulnerable.

This Psalm underscores a critical theological principle: God's unwavering commitment to justice and righteousness. It's not merely about the moral fabric of human societies but extends to every corner of creation, including the celestial realm. The meticulous care with which God oversees justice is evident. He expects those in positions of governance, whether divine or human, to act justly, protect the weak, and uphold righteousness.

By presenting this celestial court scene, *Psalm 82* also serves as a reminder to earthly leaders and authorities. Like these celestial beings, they are also accountable for their governance, and God's standard is unwavering. The principle of justice, equity, and care for the oppressed is a universal mandate, transcending both the heavenly and earthly domains.

In the pages of *1 Kings 22:19-23*, a breathtaking tableau unfolds before our eyes. Through the prophetic revelation given to Micaiah, we are granted an insider's view into the celestial chambers of the divine council. Yahweh is not depicted as an aloof ruler, disengaged from His creation in this scene. Instead, He is at the center, actively convening with the host of heaven, collectively pondering the destiny of King Ahab. What stands out in this narrative isn't just the event itself but the dynamics at play. Yahweh, while undeniably supreme, is portrayed as valuing consultation and discourse. He engages with the heavenly beings, considering their input and perspectives. Such a portrayal underscores God's nature: one that values dialogue, thinks multiple viewpoints, yet always acts in alignment with His righteous and sovereign will.

Throughout the biblical text, sprinkled here and there are these illuminating glimpses into the heavens. These narratives challenge a simplistic view of heaven as a realm of perpetual adoration. Instead, they paint a vivid picture of a heavenly court bustling with activity. Within this celestial assembly, divine entities are not just passive spectators. They are participants endowed with specific duties, responsibilities, and the freedom to play their part in unfolding God's plans. Yet, in all these engagements, their actions always orbit around Yahweh's central, unmovable authority.

Such revelations expand our theological horizons, offering a more nuanced understanding of the cosmic setup. They showcase a God who, in His infinite wisdom, has structured the heavens as a realm of order, collaboration, and purposeful governance. Far from being a solitary monarch, Yahweh is at the center of a vast network of divine beings, each contributing to the fulfillment of His grand cosmic narrative. This intricate, relational dynamic within the heavenly realm mirrors God's desire for relationship, structure, and collaborative stewardship, both above and here on earth.

Spiritual Warfare: The Cosmic Strife

The Divine Council, as delineated in scripture, provides a panoramic view into the hierarchical structure and functioning of the celestial realms. It is not just an assembly for the sake of divine pomp or ceremony but a functional gathering of divine beings entrusted with specific roles, domains, and mandates. This structured delegation serves as the backbone of the cosmic order and ensures harmonious operation under the aegis of Yahweh's sovereignty.

However, the meticulous design of this council also points to a profound vulnerability: the potential for discord and rebellion. Just as harmony in this celestial hierarchy ensures peace and order, any disruption, especially stemming from a desire for autonomy or defiance against divine authority, can have seismic consequences. In essence, it becomes evident that the very structure designed for order could, if corrupted, become an epicenter of cosmic chaos.

Several biblical passages hint at such disruptions, providing cryptic glimpses into the defection of certain members of this divine assembly. While the exact nature and details of these rebellions remain subjects of intense theological debate, the overarching narrative points towards significant disturbances in the cosmic order. For instance, texts referring to the fall of "Lucifer" or the morning star or passages that allude to the sons of God in Genesis 6 indicate that beings were initially created for divine purposes and deviated from their intended roles, challenging the authority that established them.

This divergence is not a mere celestial disagreement but the ignition points for spiritual warfare. When beings endowed with power, agency, and domain opt for rebellion, they don't just defy a higher authority; they disrupt the cosmic balance. Their rebellion introduces competing agendas, power struggles, and a battle for dominion, both in the heavens and on earth. The ensuing warfare is not confined to ethereal realms but cascades into human history, influencing nations, leaders, and spiritual climates.

The profound implications of these celestial rebellions become all the more tangible when we consider their earthly manifestations. Spiritual warfare isn't a distant, otherworldly phenomenon; it directly impacts the course of nations, the rise and fall of empires, and the spiritual well-being of individuals. The battles in the heavens find their echoes in the trials, temptations, and tribulations experienced by humanity.

The concept of the Divine Council serves as a pivotal key, unlocking profound insights into the cosmic structure and the dynamics that permeate both the heavenly and earthly realms. Rather than simply being a celestial chart detailing ranks and roles, the Divine Council provides a lens through which the complexities of spiritual warfare can be better grasped.

Firstly, understanding the Divine Council helps us appreciate the significance of hierarchy and order in the heavens. Just as earthly governments have varying roles and responsibilities among their officials, so too does the celestial realm have its divine stewards, each with designated functions. However, with these roles comes accountability and expectations, and a profound implication is herein. If these beings were to abandon their rightful duties or rebel against their divine mandate, chaos, and corruption would ensue, not just in the heavens but also on earth.

This brings into focus the origins of spiritual warfare. By acknowledging the possibility of defection within the Divine Council, we can trace the roots of the evil forces that seek to undermine God's will and disrupt the harmony of creation. Satan's rebellion, for instance, is not just an isolated incident of pride and ambition; it reflects a broader cosmic revolt, where certain members of the heavenly council chose to defy their Creator.

Furthermore, understanding the Divine Council paints a comprehensive picture of the spiritual realm's dynamics. It provides context to the spiritual battles that rage around us, emphasizing that they are not random or arbitrary but stem from a deeper cosmic narrative of allegiance, rebellion, and redemption. The forces of darkness, led by the fallen members of the council, wage war against God's dominion, seeking to distort truth, sow discord, and ensnare souls.

In essence, grasping the intricacies of the Divine Council equips believers with a more profound awareness of the spiritual realities that influence our world. It underscores the importance of spiritual vigilance and the need to align oneself with the forces of light. In understanding the celestial origins and dimensions of spiritual warfare, we are better prepared to navigate the challenges, temptations, and battles confronting us in our earthly journey.

Rebellion and Consequences: Isaiah 14 and Ezekiel 28

Isaiah 14 and Ezekiel 28 are two of the Old Testament's most perplexing and debated passages, intricately woven with allegory, prophecy, and historical reflection. Both these chapters provide invaluable insights into the theme of celestial rebellion, diving deep into the motivations and outcomes of such defiance against the divine order.

At a glance, *Isaiah 14* appears to lament the fall of the King of Babylon. However, as one delves deeper into its verses, especially in passages like *"How you have fallen from heaven, morning star, son of the dawn!"* it becomes evident that this is not just a commentary on an earthly king's demise. The language transcends the terrestrial and echoes a higher celestial being's downfall, one who was once radiant and revered. The ambitious desire *"I will ascend to the heavens; I will raise my throne above the stars of God"* reveals a heart consumed by pride and a hunger for power, hinting at a narrative that many theologians believe speaks of Satan's fall.

Similarly, *Ezekiel 28,* while initially addressing the King of Tire, uses descriptions that seem too grandiose for a mere mortal. Phrases such as *"You were anointed as a guardian cherub"* and *"You were on the holy mount of God"* point towards a being of significant divine stature. The passage paints a picture of an entity adorned in beauty and wisdom but later corrupted by its pride and splendor. This decay from perfection to iniquity further strengthens the argument that this chapter might be alluding to the tragic downfall of Satan.

Together, these two passages offer a rich exploration into the nature of cosmic rebellion. They delve into the psyche of pride, the intoxicating allure of power, and the devastating consequences of elevating oneself above the divine order. Through the laments for these kings, there's an echoing warning about the perils of pride and the inevitable judgment that befalls those who challenge the Creator.

While historical and contextual interpretations should always be considered, the profound symbolic significance of these chapters cannot be overlooked. They serve as sobering reminders of the dangers of hubris, not just for celestial beings but for humanity as well. In these poetic, prophetic narratives, we are invited to reflect on the broader cosmic drama, understanding the origins of evil, the price of ambition, and the mercy and justice of a sovereign God.

Isaiah 14: The Hubris of the Morning Star

The *14th chapter of Isaiah* opens with a prophetic pronouncement against the king of Babylon. However, as the verses unfold, the language transcends mere earthly kingship, touching upon themes that appear too grandiose for a mere mortal. The entity, described as the "morning star" or "Lucifer" in some translations, is depicted as having said, **"I will ascend to the heavens; I will raise my throne above the stars of God."**

This ambition to ascend above the "stars of God" – possibly a reference to other divine beings or members of the Divine Council – paints a picture of profound hubris. The aspiration to equal or surpass Yahweh leads to a swift denouncement: **"But you are brought down to the realm of the dead, to the depths of the pit."**

Though historical context suggests that this passage is a taunt against the Babylonian monarch, the elevated language has led many scholars and theologians to see dual implications. The audacious pride depicted here echoes a higher, cosmic rebellion, where a celestial being, endowed with beauty and splendor, sought to usurp divine authority.

Ezekiel 28: The Lament over Eden's Cherub

Ezekiel's lamentation over the king of Tyra delves even deeper into the theme of celestial rebellion. Initially described in terms familiar to an earthly ruler, the narrative takes a curious turn as it speaks of the king being in Eden, adorned with precious stones, and identified as a "cherub." This cherub is described as blameless until wickedness is found in him, leading to his expulsion from the mountain of God.

The imagery of Eden and the specific mention of a cherub extend beyond earthly realms, alluding to a being of significant celestial stature. The text paints a tragic portrait of perfection marred by free will's abuse, where a divine guardian, possibly tasked with overseeing humanity's paradise, is led astray by pride and greed.

The subsequent declaration of judgment, "I drove you in disgrace from the mount of God, and I expelled you, guardian cherub," underscores the grave consequences of such rebellion. Just as with *Isaiah 14*, the grandeur of the language and the themes explored suggest that this lament may encapsulate more than just the fall of an earthly king; it could be allegorically chronicling the fall of a significant celestial being.

Synthesizing the Rebellion: Cosmic Implications

When viewed in tandem, *Isaiah 14 and Ezekiel 28* weave a narrative of Celestial ambition, arrogance, and the ensuing judgment. While the primary focus of both chapters remains the condemnation of arrogant earthly rulers, the elevated language and imagery resonate with broader themes of cosmic rebellion.

These chapters reinforce that the Divine Council's harmony and order are not immune to discord. Even celestial beings can succumb to pride and ambition when endowed with free will, leading to catastrophic consequences. The ripple effects of such rebellions, while originating in heavenly realms, cascade onto earthly terrains, influencing spiritual climates and human destinies. Isaiah 14 and Ezekiel 28, while rooted in their historical and cultural contexts, offer profound eschatological and theological insights. By examining the possible dual implications of these texts, we gain a deeper understanding of the cosmic conflict, the nature of spiritual warfare, and the dire ramifications of rebelling against divine authority.

Dominion Over Nations: The Cosmic Drama Behind Earthly Governance

The biblical worldview is replete with a vision of heaven and earth as intricately interwoven realms. The seen and the unseen realms are not mutually exclusive but rather intricately intertwined within a cosmic fabric. Central to this interconnectedness is the role played by divine beings, particularly about earthly governance. Deuteronomy 32:8-9 and Psalm 82, among other passages, open a window into this celestial-earthly dynamic.

The Divine Distribution in Deuteronomy 32:8-9 and the Cosmic Conflict

The extensive fabric of the biblical account is intricately interwoven with elements of both the visible and the invisible, the earthly and the heavenly. Within this intricate matrix, Deuteronomy 32:8-9 stands out as a powerful testament to the delicate balance between heaven and earth, hinting at the complex choreography of the divine and human realms.

Deuteronomy 32:8-9, at a cursory glance, appears to be a historical account detailing the division of the world among nations. Yet, beneath this surface reading lies a profound cosmic reality: The Most High, in His divine wisdom, allotted nations their inheritance according to the number of the "sons of God." Such a distribution suggests a far-reaching divine strategy. It postulates a celestial blueprint where the very structure of earthly governance is predicated upon a religious order.

This segment of scripture opens up an intriguing perspective where the earth's political and territorial divisions reflect a greater cosmic scheme. Each nation was not merely handed a piece of land; it was given divine stewardship and assigned a particular member of the sacred council, the "sons of God." This celestial custodianship implies a relationship of guidance, protection, and governance, aligning the destiny of the nation with the broader purposes of the divine.

The vision Deuteronomy provides is grand in scope. It suggests that the Most High's interest and orchestration weren't limited to Israel alone. Every nation, every tribe, every language had its place in His grand design. Each divine being of the council, acting as a steward, was to shepherd its nation, guiding it along paths of righteousness, justice, and divine alignment.

However, as the biblical narrative unfolds, it becomes evident that this divinely orchestrated governance was not without its frictions. The celestial beings, endowed with authority and dominion, had the autonomy to act. Some remained faithful to their mandate, but others were lured by pride, ambition, or rebellion. Their dereliction of duty led to spiritual and moral decay, causing nations to stray from the divine path.

The resultant chaos is palpable. Nations, instead of thriving under the protective and guiding hand of their celestial guardians, were often mired in idolatry, confusion, and spiritual malaise. The divine distribution, initially a blueprint for order and harmony, became, in some instances, a platform for cosmic conflict. While originally rooted in the celestial realm, this cosmic conflict had profound implications for the earth. The rebellion and fall of some of these "sons of God" caused ripple effects, influencing civilizations, shaping histories, and defining spiritual landscapes. Their choices, driven by free will, set the stage for battles both seen and unseen.

Yet, amidst the echoes of cosmic wars and the struggles of nations, a golden thread of hope remains woven into the narrative. The true Sovereign, the Most High, remains watchful and involved. His overarching plan for redemption and restoration is never thwarted. The momentary triumphs of rebellious celestial beings are just that – momentary. In His infinite wisdom and power, the Divine continually calls nations back to Himself, seeking to realign them with His original intent and purpose.

The scriptural passage of *Deuteronomy 32:8-9* presents a multifaceted and intricate comprehension, imparting valuable perspectives on the complex interplay between the celestial and terrestrial realms. It emphasizes the profound impact of the divine sphere on the earthly domain, unveiling a divine allocation that is both influenced by and influences the decisions of celestial entities. In this cosmic intermingling of the divine and human, the ultimate aspiration lies in the unwavering designs of the Almighty, who endeavors toward the redemption and reinstatement of all His creations.

The Divine Dereliction in Psalm 82 and the elohim in Cosmic Conflict

Within the expansive scope of the biblical narrative, specific passages beckon with an allure of celestial mystery. Psalm 82 is a prime example, painting a scene of a divine assembly echoing with the tones of judgment. Here, within its poetic lines, we're afforded a glimpse into the roles and responsibilities of the elohim, or gods, and their place within the cosmic conflict that spans the ages.

As the psalm begins, we're transported to the divine council, a celestial gathering where elohim stands in God's court. These aren't mere metaphors or abstract concepts. They are genuine divine beings, part of God's cosmic administration, meant to implement justice and guide humanity. These elohim had a clear divine mandate: to uphold justice, to defend the marginalized, and to enact righteousness.

Yet, as the verses of the psalm reveal, something has gone amiss. These elohim have failed in their duties. They've shown favor to the wicked, neglected the needy, and allowed corruption to seep into their governance. This neglect hasn't just caused ripples but waves, shaking the very foundations of the world and allowing evil to flourish unchecked.

The effects of their dereliction reverberate through the realms. Their failure to act justly and uphold their divine mandates disrupts the celestial and terrestrial balance. Consequently, humanity faces the challenge of addressing moral degradation, societal inequities, and deep-seated spiritual unrest. The protective role of the elohim, designed to be a bridge between heaven and earth, now stands as a barrier, allowing chaos and darkness to proliferate.

But hope is not lost. The psalmist's voice rises amid this gloom, beseeching the Most High to act, to bring forth justice where the elohim have failed. This plea underscores a vital truth: God's sovereignty remains unchallenged. Even if the elohim falters, God's commitment to justice and righteousness remains resolute.

The climax of the psalm is both dramatic and telling. God decrees a judgment on these negligent elohim. They are said, "You shall die like mortals." They are brought down to the realm of mortality from their divine status. This isn't just punishment; it's God's way of restoring order to the cosmos. It signifies that dereliction of religious duty, even by the mightiest elohim, doesn't go unnoticed or unpunished.

In its essence, Psalm 82 isn't merely a retrospective account. It foreshadows a future where all terrestrial and celestial powers that stand against God's dominion will be dismantled. It indicates an eventual resolution to the cosmic conflict, where the disobedience of elohim and other spiritual beings will be put to an end by the unassailable authority of the Most High.

The narrative of Psalm 82 serves as a potent reminder: the allure of power, even for elohim, can lead to downfall if it's not aligned with divine justice and righteousness. Yet, even in its cautionary notes, the psalm carries a promise. Amid the complexities of the cosmic conflict and the failings of the elohim, God's sovereignty remains our anchor and His justice is our unwavering hope.

Christ's Victory and the Broader Spiritual Narrative:

Delving deeper into the New Testament, we are confronted with profound revelations about the nature and depth of spiritual warfare, mainly through Christ's redemptive mission. At a cursory glance, Jesus's death and resurrection may appear as acts of personal salvation, an intervention on behalf of individual souls. However, a more nuanced exploration reveals a cosmic scope, one that transcends the bounds of earthly redemption.

This mission wasn't merely about liberating human souls from the shackles of sin but also about wresting dominion from the corrupt and wayward members of the Divine Council. Once entrusted with significant responsibilities, these entities had, over time, twisted their roles, exerting their influence to lead nations and individuals away from the true essence of God's word.

Colossians 2:15 stands as a powerful testament to the magnitude of Christ's triumph, a moment so monumental that it resonated not just in the physical world but echoed throughout the cosmos. The Apostle Paul, in his profound wisdom and spiritual insight, draws back the curtain on this momentous event, shedding light on the vast implications of Christ's redemptive act.

When Paul speaks of "He disarmed the rulers and authorities," he employs martial and regal imagery that refers to the traditions of ancient conquerors who would parade their defeated foes in a show of power and superiority. But Paul isn't merely describing an earthly victor's parade; he's portraying the ultimate act of divine victory, where Christ nullified the powers and principalities that sought dominion over humanity through His crucifixion and resurrection.

The phrase "put them to open shame" further magnifies the scale of this triumph. It wasn't a covert victory, whispered in hushed tones. Instead, it was an open and definitive defeat, exposing these rebellious forces in their futility against God's grand redemptive plan. They were not merely defeated; they were publicly humiliated, their once-feared power now revealed as impotent against the might of Christ's sacrifice.

But the depth of this passage doesn't stop at the spectacle of victory. By emphasizing "triumphing over them in him," Paul underscores that this victory was accomplished not through brute force but through Christ's profound, sacrificial love. It's a reminder that the battleground of this cosmic conflict was not a field or a fortress but the very heart of Christ, who bore our sins, taking on the total weight of death and emerging victorious.

This passage is more than just a theological assertion; it's an invitation to comprehend the breadth and depth of Christ's love and the scope of His victory. It reiterates to believers the security they have in Christ, knowing that the forces once against them are now rendered powerless. Through Christ's redemptive act, He conquered death for Himself and broke its chains for all who believe, ensuring that they, too, could share in this grand cosmic victory.

Beyond the theological implications, this passage also reinforces the magnitude of Jesus's sacrifice. It wasn't a localized event confined to a geographical region or a specific group of people. Instead, it resonated through the multitudes of heaven, shaking the very foundations of the Divine Council and signaling a seismic shift in the balance of cosmic power. Jesus's victory on the cross stands as an eternal testament to God's steadfast commitment to restore order, justice, and righteousness, not only in the realm of humankind but across the vast expanses of His creation.

The Mantle of the Believer in the Cosmic Drama:

As we unravel the intricacies of the cosmic hierarchy and the tensions that simmer within it, the believer's role in this vast celestial narrative becomes strikingly evident. The understanding that our world, with all its visible challenges, is underpinned by an unseen spiritual battleground lends a profound depth to the believer's journey.

The Apostle Paul, in his letter to the Ephesians, eloquently encapsulates this sentiment. *Ephesians 6:12* doesn't merely offer a cautionary note but acts as a clarion call to Christians. Paul elucidates that the challenges, conflicts, and confrontations believers face are not simply terrestrial in nature. Instead, they echo a larger cosmic battle, one that pits not mere mortals against each other but places them at the crossroads of spiritual confrontations involving rulers, powers, and the formidable forces of darkness that weave their influence across the expanse of creation.

However, this realization isn't intended to daunt or overwhelm. It seeks to empower. In recognizing the magnitude of this cosmic conflict, believers also awaken to their ordained role within it. They aren't mere bystanders or passive observers. By aligning with Christ by actively choosing to walk in His footsteps, believers transition from being mere inhabitant of this world to active soldiers in God's celestial army. This isn't an aggressive role in the traditional sense but one of spiritual warriors.

Believers aren't left unequipped or unguarded as soldiers in this cosmic conflict. The divine arsenal, as elaborated further in Ephesians, provides them with an armor forged in the very heart of heaven - the belt of truth, the breastplate of righteousness, the shield of faith, the helmet of salvation, and the sword of the Spirit. Each piece is symbolic, representing the virtues, values, and verities that protect and empower believers to stand firm, resist, and push back against the insidious influences of these dark forces.

In embracing this role, believers aren't undertaking a solitary journey. They are part of a vast, interconnected network of spiritual warriors, each playing their part, each contributing to the ultimate goal: the establishment of God's kingdom, where love, justice, and righteousness reign supreme and where the shadows of this cosmic conflict are forever dispelled by the radiant light of Christ's eternal victory.

Implications for Today

The dynamics between the Divine Council and spiritual warfare have profound implications for contemporary believers:

Prayer and Intercession: Understanding the celestial battles helps believers realize the potency of prayer. Intercessory prayers become acts of partnership with God, aligning with His purposes and countering the strategies of rebellious spiritual entities.

Discerning Spiritual Climates: Recognizing that specific spiritual entities might influence regions, territories, and societal structures can guide believers in strategic prayer, evangelism, and social action.

Grounded Identity: Knowledge of the cosmic conflict gives believers a rooted identity. They are not mere mortals caught in a vast, indifferent universe but crucial players in an epic narrative aligned with the victorious side.

In summary, the Divine Council and spiritual warfare are intrinsically linked concepts that offer a broader, more nuanced view of the biblical narrative. They remind believers of the intricate, multi-layered reality they inhabit and invite them to participate meaningfully in the unfolding cosmic drama.

As we conclude our exploration of the Divine Council, it becomes evident that understanding this celestial hierarchy is fundamental to grasping the complexities of spiritual dynamics that ripple throughout both the heavenly and earthly realms. This structured order, designed for harmony and governance, ironically set the stage for one of the most profound rebellions in cosmic history. As we turn the page, we venture into an even more profound mystery that directly impacted humanity and reshaped our understanding of the celestial world. Join us in the next chapter as we delve into the enigmatic saga of the Rebellious Watchers, entities that, motivated by desire and defiance, forever altered the course of human destiny.

Chapter 3

Transgressions of the Watchers: A Deeper Dive into the Jude 6 Enigma

And the angels who did not stay within their own position of authority, but left their proper dwelling, he has kept in eternal chains under gloomy darkness until the judgment of the great day (Jude 6)

Jude 6, a mere fragment within the mosaic of the biblical text, casts a monumental shadow over the pages of spiritual history, evoking an event of such gravitas that its ripples are felt throughout the very fabric of creation. This verse shrouded in layers of mystery, serves as a potent reminder of a rebellion so audacious and unparalleled that it drew forth an earth-shattering response from the very heart of the Divine. But what was the origin of this cosmic unrest? What prompted these celestial beings—the Watchers—to forsake their lofty positions within the heavenly hierarchy? The motivations behind their actions remain cloaked in an enigma, demanding a deeper investigation. As we traverse the ancient corridors of time, retracing the ethereal steps of these divine entities, we grapple with the weighty question: What could lead beings of such majesty and purpose to set aside their religious mandates and tread a path teeming with defiance and potential doom?

The term "Watchers" itself carries a weighty sense of solemn responsibility and divine obligation. With their elevated designation, these entities were not passive observers in the grand theater of creation. Instead, they were more akin to guardians, entrusted with the task of maintaining the cosmic equilibrium and standing at the intersection of divine intentions and the unfolding tapestry of creation. Charged with upholding the grand design of the Divine, they served as silent sentinels, ensuring that the rhythm of the cosmos remained in harmony with its Creator's symphonic vision. However, in a twist that shakes the foundations of our understanding, these keepers of order became agents of chaos. What could have stirred within their celestial hearts to prompt such aberrant behavior? What passions or desires could have infiltrated beings of such purity and purpose, compelling them to defy the very essence of their existence? This mystery gnaws at our conscience, suggesting that even the most sacred of entities can be swayed by the allure of the forbidden. In their audacious act, the Watchers challenged the cosmic scheme and forced us to confront the inherent vulnerabilities even in the divine.

The towering silhouette of Mount Hermon stands not merely as a geographical landmark but as a sentinel to an epoch where celestial and terrestrial destinies are entwined. Its grandeur, reaching towards the heavens even as it roots itself in earthly terrain, made it an apt representation of the duality the Watchers were embracing. Mount Hermon wasn't simply a geographical choice—it was a declaration, a testament to their audacious journey from the ethereal heights of divinity to the tangible realm of humankind.

Throughout ancient times, mountains have always been shrouded in mystery and reverence. Their towering presence, reaching towards the heavens, has long made them symbolic of the divine, of a space where heaven and earth seem to touch. The choice of Mount Hermon by the Watchers wasn't a mere arbitrary selection but carried layers of deep significance with it.

Many ancient traditions perceived mountains as geographical landmarks and spiritual nexuses. They were believed to be bridges connecting the mortal realm with the ethereal, the profane, and the sacred. Temples, altars, and places of worship were often situated atop these elevations, further solidifying their role as mediators between the human and the divine.

Therefore, the Watchers' decision to descend upon Mount Hermon was heavily symbolic. In doing so, they were staking a claim, asserting their celestial stature while simultaneously anchoring themselves within the terrestrial realm. This act was not merely about physical transition but symbolized a theological and cosmic shift. It suggested a deliberate intertwining of the divine with the mortal, a fusion that challenged existing paradigms and spiritual boundaries.

Furthermore, the very act of descent implies intention and purpose. The Watchers were not passive visitors but active participants, keen on influencing and perhaps altering the earthly domain's course. Their arrival at such a significant location highlighted their awareness of human perceptions and beliefs. By choosing such a revered site, they were possibly seeking to leverage the existing veneration associated with mountains, thus amplifying their own influence and reception among humanity.

This melding of the celestial and terrestrial on Mount Hermon serves as a poignant reflection of the complexities inherent in the cosmic narrative. It underscores the dynamic interactions between realms, the tensions that arise from such encounters, and the profound implications these events hold for both the spiritual and physical domains.

However, this wasn't merely a benign blending of realms. The profound act of the Watchers stepping into our world was akin to piercing a veil, forever altering the equilibrium of existence. It was more than a trespass; it echoed a cosmic discord. This deliberate crossing, this audacious intermingling, sowed seeds that would burgeon into profound, far-reaching consequences, reshaping the narrative of the heavens and the earth.

The attraction the Watchers felt towards human women transcended mere physical allurements. It signified a more profound yearning, a quest for connection that bridged the chasm between the ethereal and the material. This was a confluence of the divine and the human, a melding of realms that resonated with cosmic dissonance. Such unions were not just frowned upon; they were transgressions that violated the core tenets of cosmic governance, upending the careful balance meticulously crafted by God.

The progeny of these unions, the Nephilim, embodied this breach. Their very existence defied the natural order of things. They were anomalies with a lineage tracing back to heaven and earth, standing tall as monuments to the Watchers' audacity. Their stature, both in physicality and the collective psyche, symbolized their dual heritage. They straddled two worlds, echoing the celestial might of their forefathers while being tethered to the terrestrial realm through their human lineage.

In their eyes, one could glimpse the vastness of the cosmos while their footsteps resonated with earthly weight. Their presence was a constant reminder of the boundaries that had been crossed. The Nephilim were neither gods nor men; they were the liminal beings existing in the interstices, heralding a world where distinctions between the sacred and the profane, the heavenly and the earthly, were irrevocably blurred. Through them, the world bore witness to the profound repercussions of the Watchers' choices, reminding all of the fragility of order when faced with unchecked desire and ambition.

According to the Book Of Enoch, The Watchers, in their descent, bore with them more than just their celestial essence; they carried the secrets of the heavens, enigmatic wisdom that was not meant for human consumption. Their impartation of this knowledge, whether out of a misplaced sense of benevolence or a desire to mold humanity in their image, forever altered the trajectory of human history.

This knowledge encompassed a wide spectrum — from the arcane arts to the mysteries of the cosmos. On one hand, it unveiled the secrets of metallurgy, medicine, and astronomy, propelling humanity into an age of unprecedented innovation. Cities began to rise, societies became more organized, and the frontiers of human potential expanded exponentially. With its newfound wisdom, the world seemed to stand on the cusp of a golden age.

However, every coin has its flip side. The benefits were accompanied by drawbacks. Humanity was introduced to the arts of warfare, sorcery, and manipulation. The tools meant to uplift them also became instruments of subjugation and destruction. Societies, previously united in their collective ignorance, now found themselves fragmented. The divisions weren't just territorial but also ideological. Conflicts erupted, not just over land and resources but also over the interpretation and control of this newfound knowledge.

Moreover, the sudden influx of wisdom brought with it existential dilemmas. Humanity was thrust into moral mazes, grappling with questions of ethics, purpose, and destiny. The once clear lines between right and wrong started blurring as humanity grappled with the consequences of playing with fire. The Watchers' gifts, in essence, became humanity's tests — challenges that questioned their resilience, integrity, and very nature.

In the shadow of these colossal revelations, the world transformed. The once simple, unadulterated fabric of human existence now bore intricate patterns of light and dark, an eternal dance of growth and decay, birthed from the Watchers' transgressions. In inheriting the heavens' secrets, humanity had also inherited its complexities.

Within the intricate tapestry of creation, God Almighty, in His boundless knowledge and perfect foresight, had woven a complex balance, harmonizing every element, every being, ensuring a celestial symphony of order and purpose. Yet, like discordant notes in this celestial symphony, the Watchers' rebellion introduced a tumultuous upheaval that sent ripples throughout the fabric of existence.

The Watchers, beings of significant stature and purpose, were initially entrusted with divine responsibilities. Their deviance from their divine mandate was not a mere error in judgment but a profound betrayal, a deliberate act that undermined the very foundations of the celestial order. By choosing to rebel, they disrupted the delicate balance that God had set in place, leaving shadows where there once was light.

And it wasn't just the act of rebellion that posed a grave concern. The Nephilim's birth, offspring from the Watchers' interaction with humanity, introduced a new strain of beings whose very existence was marked by a celestial and terrestrial blend. Their influence, both in might and intent, began to distort the natural order of things, perpetuating the discord initiated by their progenitors.

This cascade of events painted a bleak picture, hinting at a future where chaos might reign supreme. The foundations of the world, crafted with precision and purpose, now teetered precariously. The universe, which had always reflected God's perfection and order, was at risk of spiraling into disorder, with its original design being overshadowed by the repercussions of rebellion.

Yet, in this potential calamity, the overarching theme becomes clear: God's sovereignty and unwavering commitment to restoring balance. No act of rebellion could ever truly derail the Almighty's grand design, no matter how significant. Even as the ripples of the Watchers' transgressions spread, the narrative also hints at a Divine countermove, a plan to mend, restore, and ultimately reaffirm the glorious intent for creation. In response to this impending chaos, the Great Deluge emerged as God's profound intervention; a cataclysmic event of unparalleled magnitude, it was not just an act of destruction but also one of restoration.

The Great Deluge, an event of cataclysmic proportions, was not solely an act of devastation but also one of rejuvenation. It was as if the earth, tainted by the actions of the rebellious Watchers, needed to be cleansed and rebirthed. The waters, often symbolizing purification in ancient traditions, swept away the blemishes, including the mighty Nephilim, and offered a fresh canvas upon which humanity could rebuild, free from the immediate influences of the unsanctioned celestial-human hybrid.

Parallel to the earthly cleansing ran the heavenly trial. The Watchers, who had once graced the higher echelons of the celestial hierarchy, found themselves at the mercy of the very order they had defied. In a profound act of divine justice, these beings were bound, their luminous essence shackled and cast into the abyss. This wasn't merely a punishment but a resounding message across the realms. It underscored the inviolability of the Divine Order and the dire consequences awaiting those who dared challenge it.

At the heart of this intricate narrative lies God's multifaceted response to rebellion and disorder, operating on multiple dimensions: the terrestrial plane, with the forceful cleansing of the Deluge, and the celestial sphere, through the stern judgment passed on the Watchers. This two-pronged approach was symbolic of God's holistic vision, ensuring that every corner of His creation, visible or ethereal, adhered to His divine principles.

God's commitment to maintaining His universe's integrity, balance, and righteousness was unwavering; these events served as a potent testament to that fact. They emphasized that God's love and the freedom He granted His creations were not to be mistaken for indifference. Every being was bound by a sacred covenant, irrespective of their stature or realm. This pact celebrated free will but also emphasized the weight of responsibility that came with it.

The profound gift of free will, given to both celestial and terrestrial beings, was never meant to be a carte blanche for unbridled action. It was, instead, an invitation to coexist harmoniously within the guidelines of divine righteousness. To misuse this gift was to face immediate and lasting repercussions.

The tale of the Watchers, with its dramatic arcs and profound lessons, is a cautionary tale woven into the fabric of spiritual history. It's a timeless reminder of God's benevolence, immutable boundaries, and the profound consequences that befall those who dare to overstep. Through this saga, generations are reminded that God's universe is one of order, love, and accountability, where choices, no matter their magnitude, never go unnoticed or unaddressed.

In the post-Deluge world, as civilizations began to rise from the muddy remnants of a cleansed earth, stories and lessons of the past became invaluable. The saga of the Watchers served as both a cautionary tale and a lesson in humility for the burgeoning human populace. Every tribe, every emerging city-state would, in their own way, recount the tale of the celestial beings who traded the luminous expanse of the heavens for the tactile allure of the earth and, in doing so, altered the course of history.

This balance, so precariously teetered by the Watchers' choices, was a theme that would permeate through generations. Leaders and common folk alike would ponder the weight of duty and the siren call of desire, understanding that even the mightiest emissaries of the skies were not immune to the seductive power of temptation. The weight of responsibility and the consequences of straying from one's ordained path became central tenets in moral teachings.

And while the Nephilim no longer roamed the lands, their legacy was woven into myths, legends, and folklore. These giants of old, products of an unholy union, became synonymous with wonder and warning. They stood as a testament to the unimaginable possibilities that lay at the intersection of the human and the divine and the potential perils therein.

Yet, perhaps the most profound aftermath of the Watchers' descent was the forbidden knowledge they imparted. Whether perceived as gifts to elevate humanity or as tools of upheaval, these arcane teachings fundamentally altered the trajectory of human advancement. Novel methodologies in metallurgy, sorcery, and other disciplines emerged, driving societies into epochs of swift progress. But with innovation came disparity and moral dilemmas, forcing humanity to grapple with the ethical dimensions of their newfound wisdom. The question that would persist through the ages was clear: At what cost does knowledge come, and how does one wield it responsibly in a world forever shadowed by the echoes of celestial defiance?

The Watchers' story remains one of the most enigmatic and haunting chapters in the annals of spiritual history. Their descent, motivated by desire and curiosity, led to a series of events that forever altered the cosmic balance. It serves as a testament to the complexities of free will, the allure of the forbidden, and the profound consequences that arise when celestial boundaries are transgressed.

Implications for the Cosmic Conflict

Understanding *Deuteronomy 32's* worldview unlocks a richer perspective on the ensuing biblical narrative:

Geopolitical Strife as Spiritual Conflict:

Throughout Israel's history, it becomes evident that each confrontation, treaty, and diplomatic dance carries more than immediate concerns of land, resources, or political dominance. Beneath the surface-level geopolitics lie deeper spiritual currents that trace back to the very foundation of creation and the celestial order

Israel, chosen by Yahweh as His people, becomes the primary focal point in the material realm for this celestial struggle. Every foreign power that stands against Israel, whether it be the grand empire of Egypt, the mighty Babylonians, or the expansive dominion of Rome, doesn't merely represent a human kingdom with earthly ambitions. These empires, knowingly or unknowingly, are often depicted as being influenced or steered by spiritual entities that rebel against the true God. Hence, when Israel faces off against these nations, it's not just a battle for territory or supremacy; it's a chapter in the ongoing saga between Yahweh and the rebellious members of His divine council.

In this light, events like the Exodus from Egypt or the Babylonian Captivity take on added significance. In his refusal to let the Israelites go, the Pharaoh becomes more than just a stubborn ruler; he's a puppet in the hands of spiritual entities that oppose Yahweh's purpose for His people. Similarly, Babylon, in its conquest of Jerusalem, becomes an instrument of divine judgment, yes, but also a player in the broader cosmic drama, representing forces that stand in defiance of Yahweh's order.

Understanding this intricate weave of geopolitics with spiritual warfare elevates Israel's narrative from being mere historical accounts to profound theological statements. Their struggles against foreign powers are reframed as skirmishes in a vast, cosmic battlefield. It underscores the importance of Israel's covenantal relationship with Yahweh, as they are not just His chosen people in a geopolitical sense but also His primary allies in the great spiritual conflict that spans both heaven and earth.

It also casts a new light on Israel's leaders and prophets. Figures like Moses, Joshua, and Isaiah are not just political or spiritual leaders for their nation; they are generals and seers in Yahweh's cosmic army, receiving divine strategy to navigate and confront the spiritual entities influencing the countries around them. It brings the actual depth of their prayers, strategies, and prophetic utterances to the fore, positioning Israel not just as a nation among nations but as a central player in the grand narrative of cosmic redemption.

Idolatry as Allegiance:

According to the biblical narrative, idolatry encompasses more than the adoration of sculpted figures or adherence to unfamiliar religious practices. In the context of Israel's profound covenant with Yahweh, idolatry symbolizes a dramatic spiritual diversion—a shift in cosmic allegiance.

Israel's selection by Yahweh wasn't a simple divine preference. It was a deliberate act, designating a people for a unique relationship and communion with the Creator. This relationship was anchored in covenants, signifying adherence to divine laws and an intimate connection with Yahweh. When Israel veered towards idolatry, it wasn't merely an act of disobedience. Essentially, they were re-routing their allegiances, aligning themselves with entities that opposed Yahweh.

This broader cosmic perspective casts Israel's bouts with idol worship as more than just religious missteps. Each instance was a spiritual realignment with forces that sought to challenge Yahweh's ordained order. In *Deuteronomy 29:26,* the Israelites are admonished, "You went and served other gods, bowing down to them, gods you did not know, gods that were not given to you." This wasn't just about religious practices; it was an existential error, a declaration of loyalty with spiritual implications echoing in the heavens. Each idol, viewed through this lens, wasn't just a deity but an embodiment of an alternate spiritual narrative counteracting Yahweh's plan.

Moreover, these idols, representing varying pantheons, were often tied to the nations that stood as adversaries to Israel, both in terrestrial confrontations and spiritual realms. Thus, idol worship wasn't a mere individual or societal transgression—it symbolized national apostasy, a shift in spiritual alliances. It was equivalent to Israel publicly declaring, even if fleetingly, its willingness to turn its back on its unique relationship with Yahweh in favor of these divine adversaries.

With this understanding, the profound exhortations of the prophets take on a dimension of urgency and depth when viewed against the backdrop of the cosmic narrative. Their impassioned cries and stern warnings weren't mere ritualistic demands or calls to religious orthodoxy. They were the heartfelt expressions of intermediaries who, with divine insight, recognized the potential consequences of Israel's deviations.

The pain and sorrow expressed by God at the sight of His chosen people's repeated dalliances with idolatry was not merely a reflection of a deity slighted. It was the anguish of a loving Creator witnessing His beloved, entrusted with a unique purpose, being seduced by lesser, fleeting allurements, losing sight of their inherent role in the grand cosmic play.

The prophets, acutely aware of this larger picture, implored Israel as spiritual leaders and visionaries who could foresee the ripple effects of their choices in the spiritual realm. Their messages transcended the immediate temporal circumstances, aiming to realign Israel with their divinely ordained purpose. It wasn't merely about abandoning statues or ceasing rituals; it was about recognizing their place in a vast cosmic scheme and the weight of responsibility that came with it.

Every call to repentance, every plea for return, was steeped in a desire for Israel to understand and embrace their unique position. Amidst the cacophony of spiritual distractions and the allure of other deities, the prophets were beacons, urging Israel to remember their covenant to recognize the gravity of their actions on earthly soil and in the very heavens. Through their appeals, they sought to remind Israel that their alignment with the one true God was a matter of religious fidelity and a pivotal stance in the ongoing cosmic drama, with implications echoing throughout eternity.

Restoration as Cosmic Reorder:

At the heart of Israel's sacred narratives lies the potent theme of restoration, a longing echoed in the mournful verses of the psalmists and the fervent proclamations of the prophets. Yet, it's essential to perceive that this restoration transcends the boundaries of national revival or mere territorial reclamation. The restoration promised to

Israel isn't merely about regaining a lost homeland or reviving a glorious past; it is a profound cosmic narrative that promises the mending of the fractured universe.

The disturbances in the divine council, which began with rebellion and led to chaos in the heavens and on Earth, find their remedy in the idea of cosmic reorder. The Divine's promises, which guarantee Israel's restoration, inherently carry the weight of setting things right on a cosmic scale. It isn't merely about restoring a people but about renewing the fabric of creation itself.

When prophets like Isaiah envision a future where the wolf will dwell with the lamb and the leopard will lie down with the goat, it isn't just poetic euphoria; it's a glimpse into a reordered world where the discord of the past gives way to an orchestrated harmony. This harmony isn't limited to earthly creatures but also extends to the divine council.

The rebellious entities, the rogue members of the divine council who chose defiance over obedience, are not forgotten in this vision of restoration. The grand narrative doesn't only concern itself with their punishment but with the greater goal of harmonizing the entire cosmos. In the envisioned future, these entities will find themselves subjugated under Yahweh's dominion, not merely as defeated foes but as testamentary evidence of the power of divine order and restoration.

Thus, when we delve deep into Israel's hopes for restoration, we're invited into a grand cosmic drama where the stakes are higher than national pride or territorial gains. It is a drama where the central theme is the reclamation of order, the mending of what's broken, and the harmonizing of discordant notes into a celestial symphony, all under Yahweh's watchful gaze and guiding hand.

As we've observed, the tapestry of angelic rebellion is intricately woven with threads of cosmic mutiny, divine judgments, and humanity's inexorable link in this grand celestial drama. Such events, poignant in their significance, have left imprints not just on Earth's annals but on the very fabric of our shared spiritual consciousness. Delving into the depths of this rebellion gives us a clearer understanding of our place in the grand scheme and the forces that have sought to divert our collective destiny.

Within the intricate tapestry of biblical theology and the vast expanse of the cosmic narrative, the proclamation, *"You Shall Have No Other Gods Before Me" (Exodus 20:3)*, isn't merely a rule but a foundational principle that resonates with unparalleled depth. This mandate isn't just about whom to worship; it's a directive that anchors the people of Israel, and by broader implication, all of humanity, firmly within the universe's grand design.

The world of ancient Israel was a mosaic of cultures and religions, each with its pantheon of gods and accompanying rituals. In such a landscape, the temptation to adopt or integrate other deities into one's spiritual practices was ever-present. Yet, this commandment was a clarion call from the Divine, urging His people to remember their unique covenantal relationship and their role as bearers of a cosmic mission.

By emphasizing the importance of the one true God, this edict highlighted the intrinsic difference between Yahweh and the plethora of other deities. It was a constant reminder that God's nature, purpose, and plan for humanity were unparalleled. Every other God was a distraction, a potential pitfall that could divert the Israelites from their divine destiny.

Moreover, this commandment elucidates a more profound spiritual truth: Our choices in worship have ramifications that extend beyond the immediate and the visible. Aligning with God isn't just about personal salvation or societal harmony; it's about positioning oneself in connection with the universe's fabric. It's about understanding and embracing each individual and community's role in the unfolding cosmic drama.

Our alignment with the Divine is not a static or one-time declaration; it's a dynamic, ongoing commitment that demands awareness, discernment, and intentionality. Every act of devotion, every moment of prayer, every gesture of love and kindness becomes a stitch in the tapestry of the grand cosmic narrative. As individuals and communities navigate the intricacies of their faith journeys, they must recognize that they are not mere spectators but active participants in this vast, celestial play. This participatory role underscores the weight of responsibility on believers: to not only uphold the tenets of their faith but also to contribute positively to the broader story, amplifying the Divine's message of love, unity, and purpose in a world often riddled with confusion and chaos.

Thus, "You Shall Have No Other Gods Before Me" is not just a call to religious exclusivity. It's an invitation to partake in a divine relationship, to position oneself within the greater cosmic narrative, and to understand the profound interplay between earthly decisions and celestial consequences. In this light, the commandment becomes a compass, guiding believers through the complexities of life and ensuring their alignment with the ultimate purpose and plan of the Divine.

As we conclude our exploration of these astral renegades, it's essential to note that the stories and lessons they present are but a fragment of a broader, more mysterious universe. In a universe where realities often blur, the boundaries between the material and the spiritual frequently intersect and interact in ways beyond human comprehension. This chapter's closing doesn't signify an end but rather a gateway. It's a portal to another domain of ancient wisdom and esoteric knowledge.

In our ensuing journey, *"Demons in the Ancient Lore: Insights from The Book of Enoch,"* we will embark on a fresh exploration. The Book of Enoch, an ancient manuscript rich in myth, legend, and revelation, beckons us into its depths. It offers us glimpses into the world of dark forces, spirits that have wandered the Earth since ancient times and have whispered tales of awe and dread into the ears of generations. This next chapter promises knowledge and a deeper appreciation of the celestial dynamics that have, since time immemorial, influenced the course of human history. Join us as we navigate through these enigmatic waters, seeking clarity amidst the shadows.

Chapter 4

Demons in the Ancient Lore: Insights from The Book of Enoch

The Nephilim were on the earth in those days, and also afterward, when the sons of God came into the daughters of man and they bore children to them. These were the mighty men who were of old, the men of renown. (Genesis 6:4)

The Book of Enoch, often regarded as a pseudepigraphic work, beckons scholars and enthusiasts into a world with complex cosmology, esoteric teachings, and compelling narratives. Spanning centuries, its origin remains shrouded in mystery, giving rise to various theories about its authorship and the cultural contexts in which it emerged. This ancient manuscript, often fragmented and existing in multiple versions, offers a unique window into the religious and philosophical milieu of the Second Temple period.

Its rich tapestry of narratives—ranging from the Watchers and their interactions with humanity to Enoch's heavenly journeys—provides an unparalleled depth to our understanding of early Jewish angelology and demonology. The intricate details and vivid portrayals in the text shed light on the complexities of spiritual hierarchies, the nature of transgression, and the consequences of celestial disobedience.

While mainstream Christian theology primarily attributes the existence of demons to the fall of Lucifer and his angelic cohorts, the Book of Enoch presents a different lineage. It traces the origin of demons to the progeny of the fallen Watchers and human women, known as the Nephilim. Upon their death, these hybrid beings are said to become the evil spirits that plague humanity.

Furthermore, the Book of Enoch is a testament to religious thought's fluidity and dynamism during its time. It echoes the concerns, fears, and hopes of a society grappling with spiritual questions, seeking understanding beyond the boundaries of canonical texts. While many Christian denominations may not give it a central place in theological discussions, its influence can be felt in various apocalyptic writings and early Christian texts. For scholars and lay readers alike, the Book of Enoch serves as an intriguing bridge, connecting ancient beliefs with evolving theological paradigms and offering a deeper, multifaceted glimpse into the spiritual world of antiquity.

The Watchers and Their Transgression

The Book of Enoch introduces us to the "Watchers," a class of angelic entities that descended upon Mount Hermon and, enthralled by human women, took them as wives.

These celestial beings, driven perhaps by curiosity, fascination, or some profound yearning, descended upon the looming peaks of Mount Hermon. Their attraction to human women was not just a mere dalliance but represented a breach of the natural order, an amalgamation of the divine and the mortal. This confluence of realms resulted in repercussions echoing through the heavens and the earth.

The offspring of these unions, the Nephilim, were beings of enormous stature and strength, casting long, dark shadows upon human history. Their insatiable appetites led them to deplete the lands of their sustenance, leading to suffering and widespread famine. These giants became harbingers of despair, with their might making them virtually invincible and their very existence challenging the established order of creation.

As if the havoc wreaked by the Nephilim wasn't enough, the Watchers further entrenched their defiance by imparting to humanity knowledge meant to remain hidden within the celestial vaults. This wasn't merely knowledge for the sake of enlightenment. It was a knowledge that gave power, changed destinies, and tilted the balance of the world. From seemingly benign teachings, such as the crafting of jewelry and cosmetics, to the more malignant revelations of forging weapons and practicing dark arts, humanity was suddenly armed with abilities that it was perhaps not ready to wield responsibly.

The narrative underscores a pivotal moment in celestial history where the established harmony between heaven and earth was threatened. It paints a picture of a world on the brink, reshaped and redefined by choices born of desire and defiance.

Birth of Demons: The Spirits of the Nephilim

The account within Enoch casts a haunting shadow over our understanding of the demonic realm. Instead of introducing demons as independent, primordial entities, Enoch ties their origin to the earth that would later torment them. The Nephilim, mighty in life and terrifying in their pursuits, were doomed not to fade away quietly. Instead, they suffered a fate that seemed even more tragic than their violent existence. With the heavens refusing their admission and the earth rejecting their human form, they were rendered adrift in an ethereal limbo.

The transformation of these colossal beings into restless spirits illustrates a stark duality: Once rulers in stature and might, they became subjects of eternal punishment. Their essence, which once took from the world so voraciously, was now deprived of even the simplest earthly gratifications. This intense deprivation manifested in their interactions with humanity. The same entities that once stood tall, consuming resources, were now intangible, driven by a different form of hunger: a craving for existence, recognition, and the need to impact the living realm.

Following the destruction of the Nephilim, a belief emerged that their spirits remained—restless and bereft of the human vessels they once inhabited. According to some interpretations, these disembodied spirits transformed into evil entities are called demons. Unable to find rest and barred from the celestial realm due to the transgressions of their progenitors, they wandered the earth in a state of perpetual discontent. Stripped of their physical might, they retained deep bitterness and yearned to influence the material world. They sought to attach themselves to human hosts, not just as a means of exerting control but also as a desperate attempt to experience the tangibility and purpose they once possessed. This perspective posits that their actions are fueled by envy, longing, and a desire to reclaim a semblance of their lost identity.

In this light, their hostility towards humanity is not merely about creating chaos or asserting dominance.

Instead, their actions can be perceived as an expression of profound anguish and a relentless quest for belonging. It's as if, in their torment, they are constantly trying to bridge the chasm between their former glorious state and their current ethereal existence. Humans, being both spiritual and physical beings, represent a realm the demons once partook in and are now excluded from. This fuels their intent to interact, manipulate, and even possess humans. Their interactions become a haunting dance of seeking validation, remembrance, and perhaps even redemption. However, without clear direction or hope for restoration, their actions often manifest as destructive and evil, driven by the chaos of their fragmented existence. As humanity grapples with these unseen forces, understanding their origin and motivations could offer deeper insights into the spiritual battles that have been waged across the ages and the intricate tapestry of cosmic narratives that shape our understanding of the supernatural.

In this light, their hostility towards humanity is not merely about creating chaos or asserting dominance. It's a manifestation of their eternal angst. These are spirits marred by a profound identity crisis, oscillating between their memories of power and their present formlessness. Their interactions with humans, hence, are not just acts of malevolence but expressions of deep-seated pain and an eternal yearning for what once was.

When we delve into the stories of ancient histories, myths, and legends, striking parallels emerge. The account of the Nephilim, as presented in the Hebrew scriptures, finds curious echoes in Greek mythology and the deities of other ancient civilizations. The tale of celestial beings mating with humans and producing giant offspring is not exclusive to one tradition but seems to be a recurring motif in various cultures.

Greek mythology is replete with tales of gods and goddesses descending from the heavens, entangling themselves in human affairs, often resulting in offspring that are larger than life—both in stature and in deeds. Consider the demigods—offspring of gods and mortals. Hercules, born of Zeus and the mortal Alcmene, was renowned for his unparalleled strength. Similarly, Perseus, whose father was Zeus, and mother, Danaë, a mortal, is famed for slaying the gorgon Medusa.

In both these tales and the account of the Nephilim, these hybrid offspring possess abilities and traits that are beyond human. They stand at the crossroads of the divine and the mortal, possessing attributes of both yet fully belonging to neither realm. They embody a fusion of their divine parents' celestial power and their human lineage's earthly vulnerabilities.

Moreover, the Titans of Greek lore, formidable in their might and vastness, could be analogized to the Nephilim in terms of their immense power and the threat they posed to gods and humans. Their colossal stature and the chaos they embodied resonate with the terror that the Nephilim spread across the earth.

Outside of Greek mythology, hints of similar stories emerge. Ancient Sumerian texts speak of the Anunnaki, deities that descended from the heavens and played pivotal roles in humanity's creation and early history. The name "Anunnaki" can be translated to "those who from heaven to Earth came." Their interactions with humans and their involvement in shaping human civilization bear a resemblance to the Watchers imparting forbidden knowledge to humanity.

Drawing these parallels does more than just highlight shared stories among ancient cultures. It emphasizes a potential collective memory or shared cultural experience across civilizations. While different in detail, the stories converge on foundational themes: interactions between the divine and the mortal, the birthing of giants, and the challenges such unions pose.

However, it's crucial to approach these comparisons with caution. While parallels exist, each culture's stories are rooted in unique contexts, beliefs, and histories. Greek demigods, for instance, are often celebrated for their heroics and adventures, while the Nephilim are predominantly portrayed in a more sinister light, representing a transgression against the divine order.

In pondering these ancient tales, whether of the Nephilim, the demigods, or the Anunnaki, one is invited to reflect on the timeless human fascination with the interplay between the heavens and the earth. These stories underscore our ancestral attempt to make sense of the world, our place within it, and the ever-intriguing possibilities of what lies beyond the mortal realm.

Navigating from these hybrid offspring to the realm of demons introduces another layer of intrigue. If these tales of the Nephilim and their Greek and Sumerian lore counterparts represent a mingling of the divine and mortal, the narrative surrounding demons delves into the aftermath of such unions.

In the Book of Enoch, the spirits of the slain Nephilim became the malevolent entities known as demons, wandering restlessly and causing affliction. They are a stark reminder of the consequences of breaching the divine order, representing the residual echo of a forbidden convergence. This concept resonates deeply when we explore other cultures.

Greek mythology, for instance, speaks of vengeful spirits known as "Erinyes" or "Furies." These entities punish those who commit grave sins, paralleling the restless nature of the Nephilim spirits. Moreover, the souls of those who met tragic fates or were not given proper burial rites were believed to wander aimlessly, haunting and tormenting the living, much like the restless spirits of the Nephilim. While not directly birthed from the unions of gods and mortals, the Furies and these troubled souls represent a disruption in the cosmic balance, needing appeasement or correction.

Similarly, the Sumerian pantheon includes evil spirits, often linked to specific places or natural phenomena believed to cause harm to humans. These spirits, too, are seen as entities born out of disorder or as a result of some cosmic misalignment.

A pattern emerges when we overlay the narrative of demons arising from the Nephilim with these tales from Greek and Sumerian contexts. The mingling of heavenly and earthly realms, the giants or demigods born from such unions, and the subsequent spirits or entities resulting from their end - all these tales echo the same underlying theme: the repercussions of breaking cosmic boundaries.

Regardless of their cultural origin, these demon figures serve as cautionary symbols. They are tangible reminders of the dangers of transgressing against the natural and divine order of things. More than just creatures of lore, they embody humanity's age-old fears of the unknown and the consequences of treading forbidden paths.

In this intertwined narrative of giants, gods, mortals, and demons, we're reminded of the delicate balance that governs both the heavenly and earthly realms. These stories passed down through millennia, remain relevant because they speak to universal human experiences:

- The allure of the forbidden
- The repercussions of crossing boundaries
- The ever-present, sometimes unsettling, intersection of the tangible and the supernatural

Divergences and Implications

The Book of Enoch's account of the origin of demons stands in marked contrast to more conventional Judeo-Christian interpretations. Traditionally, demons have been equated with fallen angels, those celestial beings who, led by Lucifer, rebelled against God. Enoch, however, draws a clear distinction between the Watchers (fallen angels) and their offspring, the spirits of the Nephilim (demons). This has profound implications for our understanding of spiritual entities.

Firstly, it paints a picture of a cosmos brimming with many spiritual entities, each with its distinct origin, nature, and motivations. The Watchers, driven by desire, transgress cosmic boundaries, while their offspring, the demons, birthed from violence and subsequently disembodied, have motivations rooted in their insatiable hunger.

Secondly, the Enochian perspective lends a more tangible and earthbound origin to demons. Instead of being celestial rebels partaking in a heavenly mutiny, they are terrestrial spirits intrinsically tied to the Earth and humanity. Their head, deeply intertwined with human history, places them in direct and constant interaction with the mortal realm.

Revelation 12:4 provides a deeply symbolic narrative, and its imagery has been the subject of considerable theological discussion. The passage reads: "His tail swept down a third of the stars of heaven and cast them to the Earth. And the dragon stood before the woman who was about to give birth so that when she bore her child, he might devour it."

Many interpretations, over time, have linked this passage to the ancient fall of Satan and his angels before the creation narrative of Genesis. However, a closer examination, especially when considered within the broader context of Revelation and the New Testament, suggests this event is far more linked to the advent of Christ than to a pre-Genesis cosmic conflict.

The woman, often identified as the personification of Israel or the broader community of God's people, is about to give birth. This birth is understood to symbolize the coming of Jesus Christ into the world. The dragon, representative of Satan, is depicted as waiting voraciously to devour the child. This image can be paralleled to the attempts made by King Herod to eradicate the infant Jesus by ordering the massacre of all young male infants in Bethlehem, as detailed in *Matthew 2:16-18.*

Furthermore, the depiction of stars being cast down to Earth can be understood in a dual manner. While stars in biblical symbolism often refer to angelic beings, in this context, it might also allude to the spiritual fall and decrease of influence of many in Israel due to their rejection of the Messiah. The casting down of these stars, then, would not be a prehistoric event but a manifestation of spiritual warfare around the time of Jesus's birth.

Revelation's apocalyptic language and imagery are complex, offering layers of meaning that intersect with multiple historical events. However, anchoring *Revelation 12:4* to the birth of Christ provides a cohesive interpretation. It places the cosmic struggle right into the heart of the Gospel narrative, emphasizing the monumental significance of Jesus's arrival and the profound spiritual warfare it instigated in both heavenly and earthly realms.

Relevance to Spiritual Warfare

The Enochian perspective enriches our understanding of the cosmic drama by delving deeper into these demonic entities' origins, motivations, and operations. In the Book of Enoch, demons emerge not merely as abstract spiritual adversaries but as beings intrinsically intertwined with the human narrative. Their lineage, traced back to the Nephilim, roots them in the material realm, giving them a unique dual identity: celestial in origin yet terrestrial in their desires.

This dual nature offers insights into the intensity and complexity of their interactions with humanity. The material world isn't just a battleground for them; it's a place of yearning, a realm they are inexorably tied to due to their origins. Their profound connection to the Earth gives them a deep awareness of human desires, fears, and vulnerabilities, making their tactics more insidious.

Moreover, the idea that they view humans as both "targets" and "tools" emphasizes a more strategic dimension to their operations. They don't simply seek to oppose or torment; they aim to manipulate, influence, and harness human energies for their purposes. Their actions aren't arbitrary; they are calculated moves in a broader cosmic strategy, influenced by their history and existential cravings.

In embracing this Enochian viewpoint, one gains a richer appreciation for the intricacies of spiritual warfare. The stakes are higher, the battle more nuanced, and the lines between the spiritual and material realms more fluid than traditionally perceived. It underscores the need for heightened discernment, vigilance, and an understanding that the cosmic conflict isn't just about lofty spiritual principles and the tangible, daily realities of human existence.

Understanding these entities' nature and motivations, as Enoch gleaned, equips believers with a more nuanced approach to spiritual defense. Recognizing these spirits' earthbound hunger offers insights into how they might seek to influence, afflict, or even inhabit humans.

The Book of Enoch provides a wealth of insight concerning the celestial realm and its interactions with the terrestrial. Its account of the origin and nature of demons offers a fresh and intriguing perspective, challenging traditional narratives and inviting deeper introspection into the heart of spiritual entities and their relationship with humanity. While the book doesn't hold canonical status in most Christian traditions, its insights, particularly concerning the world of spirits, are invaluable for those seeking a deeper understanding of the spiritual realm and its implications for the living.

Implications for the Biblical Narrative

The story of the Watchers and the Nephilim provides a backdrop for understanding the state of the world leading up to the Flood. The world was marked not just by human sin but by a more profound, more pervasive corruption—a cosmic rebellion with tangible, hybrid offspring. In this light, the Flood becomes not just an act of judgment against human wickedness but a necessary measure to cleanse the Earth of these hybrid entities and the profound disorder they represented.

The presence of these entities and the backdrop of angelic rebellion also offer a more nuanced understanding of the spiritual realm. The cosmic realm is not monolithic. It is marked by hierarchies, alliances, and, as evident from the Watchers' narrative, rebellion. The battle between good and evil, order and chaos, is not just a human story but woven into the fabric of the cosmos.

Furthermore, post-flood references to beings reminiscent of the Nephilim, such as the Anakim or the Rephaim, suggest that the influence of the Watchers and their offspring didn't end with the waters of judgment. The biblical narrative, especially in the conquest accounts of the book of Joshua, carries echoes of this cosmic conflict as Israel faced and overcame these remnants.

The richly textured and deeply unsettling tale of the Watchers and the Nephilim offers a glimpse into the complex interplay between the celestial and the terrestrial. It reminds readers that the biblical narrative, centered on God's relationship with humanity, is set against a vast cosmic backdrop filled with dramas, conflicts, and rebellions.

Recognizing this dimension enriches our understanding of the ancient texts and underscores the profundity of God's redemptive work—a work that seeks to restore order, not just among humans, but across the vast expanse of His creation.

Christ's Redemption and the Victory Over Demonic Oppression

Amid life's battles and struggles, a profound narrative unfolds within the spiritual realm—one of cosmic redemption and empowerment for those who align with God Almighty. The life, death, and resurrection of Jesus Christ signify the climax of this narrative. By exploring Christ's redemptive act, believers find not just solace for the past but tools to confront and overcome the insidious forces that attempt to derail their spiritual journey.

The Power of Christ's Redemption

In the panorama of spiritual narratives, Christ's redemptive act is a beacon of hope and a testament to the unparalleled power of divine love. Beyond the evident salvation of humanity from sin, this redemptive work holds profound implications for the realm of spiritual entities, particularly demons.

The crucifixion and resurrection of Jesus Christ signify not just the defeat of death but also the disarming of spiritual principalities and powers *(Colossians 2:15)*. At the cross, Jesus secured a decisive victory over all the forces of darkness, effectively breaking their legal hold over humanity. The metaphor of "chains" poignantly captures the binding nature of sin. This oppressive force entraps humanity and, in doing so, unwittingly grants demons the legitimacy to operate in the lives of individuals. These chains aren't just literal transgressions; they represent generational curses, patterns of behavior, and the weight of shame and guilt that burden countless souls.

But the advent of Christ heralded a paradigm shift in this dynamic. Through His sacrifice on the cross, Jesus didn't merely offer a way out of sin; He decisively broke its chains. This act was more than just a demonstration of divine love; it was a forceful, cosmic statement, a spiritual declaration of victory over the forces of darkness. In this grand gesture, the legal foothold demons had over humanity—granted by humanity's transgressions—was obliterated.

For believers who accept and live in the reality of Christ's sacrifice, this means a profound transformation. The chains that once held them captive are no longer operative. Demons, once formidable adversaries wielding the chains of sin as weapons, now find themselves powerless against the shield of Christ's redemption.

However, this emancipation isn't just passive; it requires recognition and active participation. Believers must consciously choose to live in this newfound freedom, reaffirming daily that the chains of their past no longer define their present or future. Only then can they truly experience the fullness of Christ's victory over the sinister forces that once sought to oppress them.

The redemption offered by Christ does more than merely cleanse; it empowers. Believers are freed from the grip of sin and endowed with authority over demonic powers. In Luke 10:19, Jesus proclaims, "I have given you authority to trample on snakes and scorpions and to overcome all the power of the enemy; nothing will harm you." This spiritual authority, rooted in Christ's redemptive act, allows believers to resist, combat, and overcome demonic influences.

Moreover, the redemption by Christ transforms the believer's identity. They are no longer spiritual orphans susceptible to demonic deception but are adopted into God's family, bearing the seal of the Holy Spirit (*Ephesians 1:13*). This new identity acts as a shield, reducing the avenues through which demons can exert influence.

It is essential, however, to understand that while Christ's redemption offers believers power and authority over demons, exercising this authority requires faith, knowledge of God's word, and a life aligned with God's principles. Passivity or ignorance can still leave room for demonic influences, but an active, faith-filled life rooted in Christ's redemption acts as an impregnable fortress against the forces of darkness.

Christ's redemption is a game-changer in the cosmic conflict. It repositions humanity from a place of vulnerability to a position of victory. For the believer, the menacing shadows of demonic powers are dispelled by the radiant light of Christ's redemptive love, signaling freedom from oppression and the empowerment to live a life of dominion and purpose.

The Reality of Demonic Oppression

Despite the definitive victory at Calvary, believers find that the war, in many ways, has shifted to a series of guerrilla skirmishes. Knowing its time is limited, the enemy seeks to oppress, deceive, and pull believers away from their divine destiny. Demonic oppression manifests in various forms—mental torment, physical illnesses, emotional upheavals, and even generational patterns of sin.

The good news? The redemptive work of Christ didn't just deal with sin—it equipped believers with authority and tools to counteract and overcome these dark forces.

The Armor of God: Tools for Victory

Ephesians 6:10-18 outlines the Armor of God, a comprehensive set of spiritual tools that empower believers to stand firm against demonic onslaughts:

The Belt of Truth: This represents understanding and standing in the truth of God's Word. When believers ground themselves in the reality, deceptions, and lies of the enemy, they find no foothold.

The Breastplate of Righteousness: Living a life of righteousness not only pleases God but acts as a defense against accusations and fiery enemy darts.

Feet Shod with the Gospel of Peace: A life rooted in the peace of Christ and an eagerness to spread the Good News propels believers forward, taking territory from darkness.

The Shield of Faith: Embracing faith as a shield is akin to wielding an unwavering trust in the character and promises of God. This faith is not a mere intellectual agreement but a deep-seated conviction that God is who He says He is and will do what He has promised. Just as a shield in ancient warfare was designed to block and deflect the deadly arrows of the enemy, so too does the shield of faith protect believers from the insidious arrows of doubt, fear, and temptation that the adversary sends their way.

The Helmet of Salvation: In the spiritual armor, the helmet safeguards the most critical part of the warrior: the mind. Just as a physical helmet protects against lethal blows, the helmet of salvation guards the believer's mind against doubts about their salvation and the identity gifted through Christ's redemption. It constantly reminds them of the eternal security and unmerited grace they've received. With this assurance, believers can stand firm against the onslaught of despair, doubt, and fear, knowing they are eternally anchored in God's saving grace.

The Sword of the Spirit, which is the Word of God: Unlike other elements of the spiritual armor that are primarily defensive, the Sword of the Spirit serves a dual purpose. As believers wield the Word of God, it protects the enemy's deceptions and actively pierces the darkness with its illuminating truth. Each scripture, verse, and divine promise confronts falsehoods head-on, allowing believers to take an offensive stance in their spiritual battles, asserting the authority and power inherent in God's timeless Word.

Prayer in the Spirit: Essential to a believer's spiritual arsenal is the profound act of Prayer in the Spirit. This isn't merely a ritual or rote recitation; it's an intimate communion with God, where the soul transcends earthly confines to connect directly with the Divine. Through this prayerful dialogue, believers receive guidance, find renewed strength, and are reminded of their divine purpose. It serves as the vital link to the Commander of the heavenly armies, ensuring they never fight alone, always bolstered by the omnipotent presence of the Almighty.

The Name and Blood of Jesus

Two potent weapons in the believer's arsenal are the Name and the Blood of Jesus. The Name of Jesus carries the authority of Christ. At its mention, every knee shall bow (*Philippians 2:10*). The Blood of Jesus, symbolizing His sacrificial act, cleanses, protects, and stands as a testament to the enemy of the victory won. By invoking these in prayer and declaration, believers actively enforce the victory of Calvary over their lives, families, and territories.

Walking in Community

An often-overlooked tool against oppression is the power of the Christian community. The enemy seeks to isolate and target individuals. However, within a community of believers, there's collective faith, prayer, and discernment. *James 5:16* underscores this, emphasizing confession and intercession within the community as a means of healing and deliverance. This collective act not only fosters transparency and accountability within the body of believers but also fortifies them against the divisive strategies of the enemy, building a unified front in spiritual warfare.

Living Victoriously

The road to a victorious Christian life isn't about the absence of battles but understanding the victory already achieved and actively enforcing it. It involves daily suiting up with God's armor, wielding the authority in Christ's name, and immersing oneself in the transformative power of His blood. Combined with the sustenance from God's word, the guidance of the Holy Spirit, and the support of the Christian community, believers are not just equipped but empowered to overcome demonic oppression and walk the path God has illuminated for them.

The intricate tapestry of *"Demons in the Ancient Lore"* sheds light on the profound complexities of our cosmic history. As we navigate through this narrative, the intertwining stories of celestial disobedience, transgression, and their subsequent ramifications become all the more palpable. While shrouded in antiquity, these accounts have lasting echoes, influencing humanity's spiritual trajectory and our understanding of the broader cosmic order. As we transition from the haunting shadows cast by the Watchers and their demonic offspring, we move towards a more expansive arena, wherein celestial beings of varied hierarchies play their parts in a grand theater of cosmic warfare. In our next chapter, *"The Interconnection: Nephilim, Principalities, and Cosmic Warfare,"* we will venture deeper into the celestial maze, unearthing the relationships between these entities, their roles, and the far-reaching implications of their interventions in the fabric of creation. This journey promises a deeper comprehension of the universe's spiritual dimensions and an understanding of humanity's pivotal role amidst these celestial dramas.

Chapter 5

The Interconnection: Demons, Principalities, and Cosmic Warfare

For we do not wrestle against flesh and blood, but against the rulers, against the authorities, against the cosmic powers over this present darkness, against the spiritual forces of evil in the heavenly places. (Ephesians 6:12)

The mysteries of the cosmos stretch beyond the vastness of space and time, weaving into spiritual dimensions where battles of a different kind rage. In this intricate web of existence, two entities stand out in their relationship with humanity and the spiritual warfare that engulfs our world: demons and principalities. In this complex web of existence, two entities stand out in their relationship with humanity and the spiritual war that destroys our world: demons and principalities. While distinct in their operation and influence, these forces converge with the singular aim of diverting humanity from its divinely ordained destiny. As agents of chaos and deception, they collaborate in the shadows, presenting a complex challenge that requires spiritual discernment and an anchored faith for those seeking to combat their pervasive influence. Understanding their nature, origins, and interconnection is crucial to comprehending the broader context of cosmic warfare.

The Deceptive Strategies of Demons in the Cosmic Conflict

As evil entities in the cosmic landscape, Demons have a notorious history of ensnaring humanity with lies, mirages, and counterfeits. The nature of their deception is intricate, woven into both individuals' immediate, tangible experiences and broader societal and cultural paradigms. By deeply delving into biblical accounts, we unearth a more comprehensive understanding of their manipulative tactics and the profound impacts they can induce in the broader cosmic conflict.

1. The Garden of Eden and the Genesis of Deception (Genesis 3)

The encounter in the Garden of Eden between the serpent and Eve stands as a pivotal moment in the biblical narrative, marking not only the tragic introduction of sin into the human experience but also offering a profound lesson in the art of deception. The serpent's approach was nuanced and cunning. Instead of presenting an outright lie, he wove a tapestry of half-truths, casting aspersions on God's intentions and words. By posing questions like "Did God really say...?", the serpent sought to instill a seed of doubt in Eve's mind, making her question the very nature of God's command and His purpose. It's a chilling reminder that the most effective lies are often those closely intertwined with elements of truth. The subtlety of this deception serves as a testament to the methods employed by demonic entities. They don't always resort to blatant falsehoods. Instead, they can craftily lead individuals down a rabbit hole of questioning, skepticism, and, ultimately, rebellion. Such deceptions are dangerous precisely because they don't appear as deceptions at first glance but rather as mere ponderings or innocent queries. Over time, these seemingly benign doubts can grow, pulling one further away from truth and light and leading them unknowingly onto a path of spiritual compromise. This subtle drift often occurs unnoticed, with the individual rationalizing or dismissing the minor deviations from their foundational beliefs. As the distance widens, the protective barrier of faith weakens, making one more susceptible to the manipulations and deceptions of these evil forces.

2. The Wilderness Temptation: A Clash of Kingdoms (Matthew 4:1-11)

The temptation of Jesus by Satan in the wilderness is a monumental moment in the New Testament, illustrative of the cosmic clash between the kingdom of light and darkness. This was not a mere test of wills but a profound theological and cosmic standoff. In offering Jesus, the kingdoms of the world, Satan was essentially challenging the preordained redemptive plan set forth by God, trying to find an alternate route to derail God's mission.

The devil's employment of Scripture to tempt the Savior reveals an alarming tactic in the arsenal of demonic deception: using truth as a conduit for falsehood. By quoting Scripture out of its intended context or with a twisted interpretation, Satan sought to weaponize the very words meant for life and liberation. This act unearths a disturbing realization: even sacred truths can be manipulated for nefarious purposes.

For believers, this underscores the importance of deeply understanding and rightly dividing the Word of God. It's not sufficient to merely know Scripture; one must also understand its context, heart, and application. The enemy knows the Word, but he doesn't adhere to its spirit. Therefore, believers are called to be not just listeners or readers of the Word but diligent students, ensuring they are equipped to recognize when sacred scriptures are being misused as tools of deception. This incident with Jesus serves as a potent reminder that discernment is crucial in navigating the spiritual battles that rage, as the line between truth and illusion can sometimes appear razor-thin.

3. Possession: The Blurring of Identity (Mark 5:1-20)

The account of the Gerasene demoniac stands as one of the most harrowing depictions of demonic possession in the biblical canon. "Legion," a horde of unclean spirits, had so thoroughly subjugated the man that his essence, humanity, was overshadowed. No longer was he recognized by his name or past; he was defined by the chaos and pain that consumed him, wandering the tombs in isolation, a pariah in his own land.

Such extreme instances of demonic influence serve a dual purpose in the grander scheme of cosmic warfare. Firstly, they vividly showcase these malevolent entities' corrupting and dehumanizing intent. Demons are not merely content with causing distress; they aim to obliterate the divine image in individuals, reducing them to mere shadows of their God-intended selves. In their relentless pursuit, they weave a web of deception, preying on vulnerabilities and seeking every opportunity to sever the soul's connection with its Creator.

Secondly, by manifesting so overtly in a person, demons can manipulate the collective psyche of a community. The sight of a possessed individual, especially one as tormented as the Gerasene demoniac, sows' seeds of terror and superstition. Such fear can spiral, leading to myths, misconceptions, and an overemphasis on the power of the demonic, sometimes to the point where God's sovereignty is questioned.

These acts of puppetry, where individuals are made marionettes in the hands of evil spirits, are not just about possessing a single soul; they are strategic plays intended to skew perceptions and mislead many. They become cautionary tales for believers, reminders of the depths of deception and the importance of discernment and vigilance in the face of evil.

4. Doctrinal Deception: The Corruption of Belief (1 Timothy 4:1-2)

Paul's letters to Timothy show a palpable sense of urgency, almost akin to a watchman sounding an alarm before an impending onslaught. With the foresight afforded to him through the Spirit, Paul glimpses into an epoch where the sanctity of the Church's teachings would be under siege. These aren't mere forebodings of external threats but of insidious infiltrations of wolves cloaked in sheep's clothing.

Deceptive spirits working their treachery through doctrinal distortions present one of the most subtle yet profound dangers to the Church. Unlike overt demonic possessions or apparent oppositions to God's work, these deceptions blend in, making them far more difficult to discern. They work by embedding false truths within genuine doctrines, muddying the waters of orthodoxy.

The consequences of such infiltration are manifold. Firstly, by skewing core teachings, these spirits dilute the Gospel's transformative power. When foundational truths are altered or denied, the very essence of faith gets compromised, potentially leading believers astray and into spiritual jeopardy.

Secondly, doctrinal deceptions become catalysts for division within the Church. Disagreements over teachings can lead to schisms, fragmenting the body of Christ. Fueled by demonically influenced doctrines, such divisions weaken the Church's collective witness and make it susceptible to further deception and external threats.

Moreover, Paul's warnings remind us that the battle believers wage is not just in the realm of the personal but in the collective. The doctrines and teachings of the Church are the bedrock upon which faith communities stand. If these are compromised, it creates an unstable foundation, jeopardizing the spiritual health of countless believers. Hence, the call is not just for individual discernment but for communal vigilance, ensuring that the faith remains uncorrupted and pure once delivered to the saints.

5. *The Broader Strategy: Societal and Cultural Manipulation*

The modus operandi of demonic forces extends beyond singular, isolated events. Their insidious intent manifests in sweeping campaigns that seek to recalibrate the foundations upon which societies are built. The domains of culture, politics, and philosophy are not mere human constructs; they are the battlegrounds upon which these forces operate, embedding and nurturing ideologies that deviate from God's truth.

With its influential grip on the mass psyche, culture becomes a potent tool in their arsenal. Through art, music, literature, and even social customs, these forces can infuse values that are diametrically opposed to divine principles. Over time, these values can crystallize into cultural norms, leading societies to embrace behaviors and beliefs that are incongruent with God's design while viewing them as simply "the way things are."

In the political arena, demons can influence policies and governance styles, promoting systems that oppress, divide, and marginalize. The rise of unjust rulers, enacting policies that perpetuate inequality, or propagating divisive ideologies can often be traced back to this evil influence, which seeks to establish realms of chaos and discord.

The philosophical realm, meanwhile, offers these entities a platform to challenge and distort fundamental truths about existence, morality, and the divine. Influencing key thinkers or popularizing certain philosophical leanings can lead societies into existential crises, moral relativism, or even atheistic inclinations.

The tragedy here is the subtlety with which these deceptions operate. They often go unnoticed or unchallenged because they are embedded within the very fabric of societal structures. Generations grow up internalizing these falsehoods, viewing them not as deceptions but as self-evident truths. This normalization of deceit underscores the imperative for discernment and the constant anchoring in God's unchanging truth, lest societies drift into oceans of illusion, mistaking the waves of falsehood for solid ground.

In the Cosmic Theater: An Ever-evolving Strategy

Having borne witness to the vast epochs of human history, Demons have adeptly adapted their tactics to suit changing circumstances and cultures. As they observed humanity's transition from nomadic tribes to enormous empires and from agrarian societies to industrialized nations, these evil entities have recalibrated their approaches to exploit the vulnerabilities of each era best. In antiquity, their interference was often manifested through overt possessions, curses, or confrontations, leveraging the prevailing superstitions and beliefs of the time.

However, as humanity transitioned into the Age of Reason and the subsequent modern era, these entities discerned the shifting sands of the human psyche. Realizing that overt displays might not always be effective in an age of skepticism, they began to weave their deceptions into the ideologies, philosophies, and cultural narratives that define societies. Instead of blatant possessions, they now sow seeds of discord, mistrust, and falsehood within institutional frameworks, media narratives, and educational paradigms. Their subtlety is their strength, as they mask their deception under the guise of progress, enlightenment, or even freedom.

73

Yet, for all their adaptability, their central aim remains unaltered: to lead souls astray, causing spiritual destruction and disconnection from the divine. But humanity isn't defenseless. As believers grow in understanding of these ancient adversaries, they're better equipped to discern and resist. Armed with the Word of God and the wisdom it imparts, believers can navigate the intricate maze of modern life, identifying and countering the subtle snares set by these entities. The battle may be unending, but with vigilance and faith, the believer can stand resolute, a beacon of truth in a world often shrouded in illusion.

While demons often operate on a personal and immediate level, manifesting in individual lives and localized occurrences, the scope of the spiritual warfare extends far beyond these entities. Principalities, a higher echelon of spiritual beings, play a more overarching and strategic role in the cosmic battle. Operating from the shadows, they influence regions, ideologies, and even epochs. These entities represent a broader, more systemic level of spiritual warfare, targeting not just individuals but entire communities, nations, and generations. As we shift our focus from the ground-level tactics of demons, it becomes essential to understand the aerial maneuvers of these principalities and the profound influence they wield in the unseen realms.

Principalities and Powers in the Cosmic Conflict

This realm, though invisible to the human eye, intersects and influences This realm, though invisible to the human eye, intersects and influences our tangible world in profound and often underappreciated ways. The Bible elucidates a vibrant, dynamic cosmic community with its dramas, alliances, and conflicts. Within this framework, the "principalities and powers" are not merely abstract concepts but active, sentient forces. These are not just rank-and-file angels; they occupy significant positions of authority and dominion in the spiritual echelons.

- Paul's writings, especially in Ephesians, provide:
- Insights into these beings.

- Hinting at their role in influencing human affairs.
- Governing territories.

Even shaping the ideologies and philosophies of entire societies.

The tug-of-war between light and darkness, good and evil, is not just an individual's inner struggle but is played out on a grand cosmic scale, with these entities at the forefront. Understanding their nature, influence, and tactics is crucial for believers, as it equips them to better navigate their earthly journey's spiritual challenges and engage effectively in the battles of faith.

Nature and Hierarchy:

In the New Testament, the terms "principalities" (archai) and "powers" (exousiai) surface as critical elements in the intricate spiritual landscape. These terms aren't used casually; they offer a glimpse into the layered hierarchy of the spiritual realm, revealing entities that hold profound positions of influence. These "principalities" and "powers" aren't typical supernatural beings that one might encounter in folktales or popular culture. Instead, they are depicted as celestial rulers with considerable clout, sitting high atop the spiritual ladder.

Their roles in the cosmic scheme are expansive. Rather than focusing on isolated events or individuals, these principalities and powers orchestrate larger spiritual campaigns, setting the spiritual tone for entire regions or nations. When we speak of the spiritual climate or atmosphere of a place or time, we often unknowingly refer to the influence of this archai and exousiai. Their reach isn't confined to isolated pockets of activity; they can shape epochs, guiding or misguiding entire generations based on their objectives.

Understanding this broad-reaching influence of principalities and powers is crucial. It reframes our understanding of spiritual warfare, moving it from merely personal struggles to encompassing broader societal and historical dimensions. Recognizing their influence empowers believers to address individual challenges and discern and counteract the more extensive spiritual narratives at play in the world around them.

Operations and Strategies:

Principalities and powers are the architects of spiritual stratagems that impact entire nations and civilizations. Their influence is not merely opportunistic but meticulously planned, targeting the moral and ethical foundations of societies. When we witness pervasive philosophies that negate the sanctity of existence or when institutions seemingly uphold inequalities, it's often a testament to the workings of these shadowy figures. Their dominion is not bound by geography or time; they've been orchestrating these grand deceptions throughout history.

In his letter to the Ephesians, Paul doesn't just mention these entities in passing. His deliberate callout in Ephesians 6:12 serves as a crucial reminder to believers. It's a call to awareness, revealing that our daily struggles and systemic issues have a deeper spiritual dimension. These principalities and powers don't operate overtly; they prefer subterfuge, embedding their lies and rebellions within societal norms and values. This stealth approach allows them to sway hearts and minds massively, steering humanity away from God's original design. Recognizing this influence is the first step in resisting and combatting the insidious agendas they propagate.

Historical Manifestations:

From ancient times to the present day, the annals of history are marked with empires, ideologies, and cultural trends that defy the wisdom and intentions of the Divine. These aren't mere coincidences or the simple result of human evolution and development. Behind the meteoric ascent of certain heretical doctrines, the emergence of autocratic systems, and the crafting of societal standards that conflict with God's mandates, a more sinister and coordinated effort is at play. Principalities and powers operating from the spiritual realm are often the driving forces behind such global shifts.

These entities, deeply entrenched in their rebellion against God, have mastered the art of using human ambition, fear, and desire to further their agendas. By influencing key leaders, inspiring foundational philosophies, or molding cultural narratives, they can subtly redirect the trajectory of entire civilizations away from godly truths and towards paths that serve their disruptive purposes. In many ways, the grand tapestry of human history, with its wars, revolutions, and ideological battles, reflects the unseen warfare between these principalities and the forces of Heaven, vying for the souls and allegiances of humanity. Recognizing their handiwork requires discernment, for one can only begin to counteract their profound influence on the world stage.

Understanding this hidden dimension of history provides a deeper perspective on past events and equips believers for present and future challenges. Every era presents its unique battles, but the underlying strategies of these spiritual entities remain consistent: sow discord, propagate deception, and pull humanity away from its Divine purpose.

Countering Their Influence:

Given their significant influence, it might seem daunting to counteract the operations of these spiritual entities. However, the New Testament offers hope. In Colossians 2:15, Paul speaks of Christ having "disarmed the principalities and powers," making a public spectacle of them through His triumph on the cross. This victory of Christ ensures that, while these entities might rage, their ultimate defeat is guaranteed.

For believers, the call is to stand firm in faith, equipped with spiritual armor, and to challenge these systemic evils through prayer, righteous living, and the proclamation of the Gospel. The influence of principalities and powers can be resisted and diminished by shedding light on dark places and aligning societal structures with divine truths.

Understanding the role of principalities and powers in the cosmic conflict equips believers to perceive the broader spiritual implications of world events. It emphasizes the need for a united, strategic, and emotional response from the Church to confront these age-old adversaries effectively.

Principalities, as described in spiritual literature, exert substantial influence over the collective psyche and direction of societies. Operating in the unseen realm, these entities hold sway over cultural, political, and social systems, subtly orchestrating thought patterns, norms, and value shifts. Their impact can be discerned in the rise and fall of ideologies, the formulation of societal norms that diverge from universal truths, and the collective consciousness of entire nations. Often, their influence perpetuates systems of injustice, fuels divisive narratives, and encourages values that are antithetical to holistic well-being and spiritual alignment. Understanding the role of principalities is vital for discerning the deeper spiritual dynamics at play behind societal trends and events. Let's take a look at some examples.

Guardians of Territories:

One of the most prominent roles of principalities and powers is their guardianship over specific territories or nations.

● *Celestial Patrons:* Just as nations today have leaders or representative figures, territories, and nations have patron entities in the spiritual realm. Depending on their alignment with divine will, these entities act as protectors, influencers, or even oppressors. The interplay between these spiritual patrons and their earthly counterparts can significantly influence the spiritual, moral, and even political trajectory of the regions they oversee, making the spiritual realm an essential consideration in understanding global dynamics.

● *Spiritual Diplomacy:* In places like the book of Daniel, we gain insights into the interactions between these territorial spirits. For instance, the "prince of Persia" resisted a messenger angel sent to Daniel, indicating that these entities have realms of influence and can engage in spiritual 'diplomatic' skirmishes. Such encounters underscore the intricacies of the spiritual realm, revealing that cosmic battles are being waged behind the curtain of our physical reality that can directly impact the course of human events and prophetic timelines.

Architects of Systems:

Principalities and powers exert their influence by shaping the world's systems, ideologies, and structures.

- **Societal Molders:** From political ideologies and cultural norms to economic practices, these spiritual entities can influence, directing them toward God's intent or away from it. For instance, oppressive systems that thrive on injustice, inequality, or prejudice might be under the sway of these adversarial powers. Their influence can be so deeply woven into the fabric of society that challenging these systems can often feel like confronting an immovable force, emphasizing the need for both spiritual discernment and divine intervention.

- **Cultural Trendsetters:** These entities can subtly nudge the trends, philosophies, and even artistic directions of a society. They can direct masses towards or away from divine truths by shaping popular culture and thought. Their subtle manipulations can become deeply ingrained, making deviations from God's principles seem normal and desirable, further obscuring the path to genuine enlightenment and connection with the divine.

Tempters and Accusers:

On a more personal scale, these spiritual forces play roles that directly impact individual spiritual journeys.

- **Enticers to Rebellion:** Principalities and powers can function as tempters, drawing individuals away from the path of righteousness. This can manifest as doubts, desires against divine principles, or even enticements that lead to morally compromising situations. Moreover, their influence can be so pervasive that individuals often mistake these temptations for their own thoughts or genuine desires, making resistance even more challenging.

- **Spiritual Prosecutors:** Once individuals succumb to these temptations, the same entities can turn accusers, leveraging guilt, shame, and condemnation to distance them from the divine presence.

They aim to entrap souls in a cycle of sin and self-condemnation, making reconciliation with God seem insurmountable. This relentless barrage of accusations drowns out the voice of hope, ensuring that individuals remain isolated and overwhelmed by their transgressions.

Gatekeepers of Forbidden Knowledge:

In specific interpretations, some of these entities hold and occasionally dispense forbidden or esoteric knowledge to humanity, often leading to consequences. Their aim is not enlightenment but entrapment, leading society down paths that promise power but deliver spiritual bondage.

- *Guardians of Esoteric Information:* Some entities are believed to possess and sometimes reveal secret or forbidden knowledge to humans, though with often detrimental outcomes.

- *Deception Through Promise of Power:* Their primary intent isn't genuine illumination but ensnarement, luring individuals with the allure of power and knowledge only to trap them in spiritual chains.

Challengers to Divine Authority:

Regardless of their specific roles, these entities ultimately share a common agenda: challenging and undermining the divine order.

- *Opposition to Divine Movements:* They resist manifestations of divine will, whether it's the spread of divine truths, the emergence of spiritual awakenings, or the establishment of justice and righteousness. Their actions often manifest as obstacles or hindrances in the paths of prophets, spiritual leaders, and believers seeking to thwart or dilute the impact of positive spiritual movements.

- *Perpetrators of Spiritual Blindness:* They aim to cloud spiritual perception, ensuring that individuals and societies remain unaware of the deeper spiritual realities, making them easier to manipulate and control. By obscuring these truths, they can steer hearts and minds more effectively away from divine enlightenment, fostering reliance on worldly understanding and leading many astray.

In their diverse roles, the principalities and powers act as both influencers and obstacles in the grand cosmic narrative. Their influence permeates realms, systems, cultures, and individual lives. But this revelation isn't meant to induce fear. Instead, understanding their operations enables believers to be vigilant, discerning, and proactive, ensuring that they remain aligned with God in every facet of life and resist adversarial forces that seek to divert them from their spiritual destinies.

The Cosmic Clash: Evangelism Against Principalities

Within the expansive panorama of the cosmic struggle, the potency of principalities assumes a prominent role, directing communities, molding belief systems, and exerting sway over the populace. Yet, in this formidable theater of spiritual warfare, a singular act has the power to disrupt, challenge, and reclaim territory from these dominions: evangelism. The proclamation of the Gospel is not merely about individual salvation; it's a radical act of defiance against these unseen rulers, ensuring that with every soul won for Christ, their territories diminish.

At its most fundamental level, evangelism revolves around the intimate act of connecting with an individual soul. While deeply personal, the decision to accept the Gospel has repercussions that resonate far beyond a single heart. Indeed, every conversion stands as a profound affirmation of the Gospel's transformative power. But the implications stretch even further. In the vast, unseen battleground where principalities exert dominion, each soul that embraces Christ chips away at its stronghold. It's akin to a breach in a seemingly impregnable fortress, marking the beginning of its downfall.

Moreover, the impact of this individual transformation doesn't stop with the person. Like a stone thrown into a pond, the ripples spread outward. Families witness the change and are often moved, communities begin to feel the influence of this newfound faith, and before long, entire societies can find themselves reshaped, reframed, and realigned closer to the values of the Kingdom of God.

The extensive fabric of historical records bears witness to this particular phenomenon. Countless revivals, reformations, and spiritual awakenings trace their origins to the authentic conversions of a few genuine individuals. Once ignited, this fire of faith becomes contagious, challenging the principalities' carefully constructed facades and paradigms. It spreads with fervor, illuminating the shadows and weakening the hold of these spiritual adversaries over individuals and communities.

The Apostle Paul, writing to the early church, often emphasized the cosmic dimensions of their faith journey. The narrative was always bigger than the immediate persecution or internal discord challenges. They were, in essence, frontline soldiers in a battle of cosmic proportions, where every act of faith, every testimony, and every soul won for Christ signified a victory in the heavenly realms.

This perspective reframed their daily struggles and put into context the significance of their testimonies. Instead of viewing their experiences as isolated incidents or coincidences, they began to understand their lives as part of a divine plan woven through history. Every prayer, every outreach, and every act of love was not just about earthly impact. Still, it echoed in eternity, directly countering the strategies and plans of the principalities and powers. Their faith was not merely about personal salvation but about participating in a grand narrative that would shape the destiny of the cosmos.

But how do principalities lose their grip through evangelism? At a fundamental level, their power thrives on deception, division, and darkness. These shadows are dispelled when a person encounters the pure light of the Gospel. Old lies are exposed. The chains of previous generational beliefs and cultural deceptions start breaking. As more and more individuals experience this liberation, communities' collective consciousness begins to shift. Principalities, which once held sway over entire cultures or societal structures, find their grip weakening.

Furthermore, each newly converted believer becomes an ambassador for Christ, equipped and commissioned to penetrate the territories further once held by these spiritual adversaries. The spiritual gifts endowed upon them—prophecy, teaching, healing, discernment, and more—become tools to dismantle the fortresses of falsehood further. Evangelism is not just about saving souls; it's about reclaiming territories from the enemy and establishing God's kingdom on earth as it is in heaven.

In this grand narrative, every believer has a pivotal role. Armed with the truth, motivated by love, and powered by the Holy Spirit, they march forward to win souls and establish a reality where principalities are dethroned, and Christ reigns supreme.

Navigating the intricate landscape of spiritual warfare requires a deep understanding of both demon's and principalities' roles. With humanity often standing at the intersection of these cosmic battles, discerning the strategies of these spiritual adversaries becomes vital. As we conclude our exploration of demons, principalities, and their shared agenda in cosmic warfare, our journey takes us deeper into the mysteries of the ancient world. In our next chapter, we'll examine the significance of these legendary beings and how their existence and legacy might illuminate our understanding of the prophetic end times.

Chapter 6

Nephilim and the Cosmic Conundrum: The Days of Noah and the End Times

For as were the days of Noah, so will be the coming of the Son of Man. For as in those days before the flood they were eating and drinking, marrying and giving in marriage, until the day when Noah entered the ark, and they were unaware until the flood came and swept them all away, so will be the coming of the Son of Man. (Matthew 24:37-39)

The richness of the biblical narrative unfolds with intricate details, many of which invite a keen-eyed seeker to delve deeper into its woven mysteries. The cultural backdrop of the ancient Near East provides a lens, magnifying these hidden elements. Among the most enigmatic of these details is the reference to the Nephilim in Genesis 6. These beings, shrouded in antiquity, become even more significant when we consider Jesus' prophetic words in *Matthew 24:37-39,* where He declared that the end times would mirror the days of Noah. Such a comparison isn't merely about historical cycles or patterns; it implies a recurrence of cosmic battles and unseen spiritual dynamics. By understanding these parallels, we might unlock profound insights into the culmination of salvation history and the eschatological events awaiting humanity.

Each narrative within the Bible, ranging from the ostensibly uncomplicated to the profoundly enigmatic, fulfills a specific function within the broader fabric of God's overarching story. For centuries, theologians, historians, and laypersons have pondered the mysteries of these ancient texts. The Nephilim, often viewed with fascination and trepidation, exemplify the Bible's capacity to engage its readers in profound theological contemplation. Delving into the world of the ancient Near East, we encounter a milieu teeming with myths, legends, and supernatural entities that resonate with biblical accounts but also diverge in significant ways. The Nephilim, as depicted, muddies the distinction between the divine and the mortal. This blurring becomes especially pertinent when juxtaposed with Jesus' prophetic utterances, hinting at an end-time scenario echoing the complexities of Noah's era. As the past and future converge in these prophecies, believers must brace themselves for unprecedented spiritual challenges. It underscores the necessity of discernment, vigilance, and an unwavering commitment to divine truths in navigating the impending spiritual storm.

Echoes of Noah's Time in Jesus' Warnings

When Jesus invokes the imagery of the "days of Noah" in His Olivet discourse (*Matthew 24:37*), He isn't merely offering a historical comparison; He's hinting at a wealth of theological and esoteric knowledge, packed into a brief allusion. This reference could be seen at the surface level as an analogy to the widespread moral decay and divine judgment that characterized Noah's time. However, when one pierces through the veil of the broader narrative, there's a resonance with the enigmatic presence of the Nephilim and the intricate web of cosmic disturbances surrounding them. The era preceding the flood was characterized by human malevolence and celestial disturbances, leading to a melding of the divine and the mortal realms. By pointing to this epoch, Jesus may be signaling the convergence of spiritual, moral, and even supernatural crises in the times preceding His return, urging His followers to be vigilant and discerning.

The societal degradation and moral bankruptcy that marked Noah's era provide an unmistakable blueprint for understanding end-time prophecies. Yet, to reduce Jesus' reference to mere ethical deterioration would be a profound oversimplification. Human transgressions didn't just characterize the world of Noah, but it was teetered on the precipice of supernatural intrusions and celestial imbalances. Jesus, with his profound insight, might be indicating that as the end times approach, humanity won't just grapple with its internal moral failings. Instead, the world could witness heightened supernatural activities reminiscent of those perplexing events before the flood. This potential resurgence serves as a clarion call for believers to be morally vigilant and spiritually discerning, prepared to navigate a landscape where the cosmic and earthly realms intertwine in unpredictable ways.

Humanity's moral descent did not simply mark this era but was also rife with cosmic aberrations that disrupted the divinely ordained order. For Noah and his contemporaries, these disruptions might have seemed impossible. Yet, the response of most was indifference or obliviousness. They were consumed with the everyday affairs of life—eating, drinking, marrying—despite the colossal shadow that the Nephilim and the moral decay they represented cast upon the earth. When it came, the flood was not an arbitrary act of judgment but a necessary intervention to reset a world that had spiraled out of balance.

In the New Testament, when Jesus warns of the forthcoming days echoing the days of Noah, His words unfold a multidimensional cautionary tale for His followers. At first glance, this warning is a straightforward reminder about the dangers of becoming lethargic amidst the glaring moral degradation that will characterize the end times. It serves as a call for believers to maintain their integrity and not get swept away by the tides of societal decadence.

However, delving deeper into Jesus' pronouncement reveals layers of nuance beyond moral decadence. The days of Noah weren't marked only by societal wrongdoing; they were tainted by profound supernatural disruptions and anomalies, signaling a deeper undercurrent of cosmic rebellion. The allusion to a similar period returning implies that the end times will encompass more than just human ethical decline; it may also witness a significant intertwining of the natural and the supernatural realms. Just as Noah faced challenges that transcended human comprehension, believers in the end times might be confronted with spiritual complexities that demand heightened discernment, faith, and reliance on divine guidance. This perspective underscores the necessity for believers to be ethically and spiritually rooted, fortified against the multifaceted challenges of the prophesied times.

Likewise, the end times could usher in unique supernatural trials. While the manifestations might vary from those experienced during Noah's era, their potential to mislead, destabilize, and veer away from divine truths will persist. It's imperative for believers to not only uphold moral integrity amidst societal decay but also to cultivate a sharp spiritual insight capable of recognizing these celestial disturbances. This enhanced discernment will be vital in traversing the complex spiritual terrains of the end times, guaranteeing that one stays rooted in truth amidst earthly and otherworldly deceptions.

As such, the call to action for present-day followers is not limited to maintaining ethical integrity alone. It involves cultivating a deep spiritual sensitivity that can pinpoint and counteract these cosmic shifts. It necessitates remaining vigilant, not only toward the glaring signs of moral degradation but also towards the subtle ripples of supernatural influences. Much like how Noah was instructed to craft an ark in preparation for the impending flood, today's believers are equipped with divine tools—like faith, prayer, and holy scriptures—to navigate the intricate spiritual dynamics of the end times. They are beckoned to remain proactive, holding steadfast against the multifaceted challenges posed by earthly temptations and celestial forces, threatening to disrupt God's ordained purpose for creation.

Moreover, this spiritual journey isn't one to be taken lightly. Just as the ark was a refuge amidst the deluge, the spiritual tools provided by God act as shields against the overwhelming tide of end-time challenges. Beyond the literal interpretation of scriptures, these tools symbolize the divine wisdom, protection, and guidance available to believers. Embracing them wholeheartedly not only aids in discerning truth from deception but also empowers believers to act as beacons of hope in an increasingly chaotic world.

History has shown us that when the lines between the physical and metaphysical become blurry, societies often grapple with existential crises and a deep spiritual hunger. These moments of collective introspection offer believers a unique opportunity to step up as torchbearers of truth, leading by example and demonstrating the transformative power of divine love. In doing so, they resist the pull of celestial adversaries and create sanctuaries of faith, hope, and love amidst the storm, echoing the refuge that Noah's Ark provided in its time.

It's worth noting that the onus isn't solely on individual believers. Communities of faith, churches, and spiritual assemblies play a crucial role in fostering collective spiritual discernment, creating support networks, and disseminating knowledge essential for navigating the end times. These communities stand as bulwarks against the tide of confusion, reinforcing the timeless message that God's plan and purpose will ultimately prevail even in the face of immense adversity.

The Nature of Archetypes

Archetypes, conceived in theological and literary domains, are foundational templates—timeless symbols or themes that recur across cultures and epochs. They encapsulate universal truths, experiences, or phenomena, presenting them in characters, stories, or motifs. The concept of the Nephilim as an archetype, especially concerning the end times, is an intriguing proposition. It implies that these ancient beings, with their distinct attributes and the circumstances surrounding their existence, serve as a symbolic prototype or precursor for future events or manifestations.

Reflecting upon the Nephilim in this light is not about expecting a literal resurgence of giant beings. Instead, it's about concerning the essence of what they represented—a convergence of the divine and human, a distortion of ordained boundaries, or perhaps, a manifestation of profound cosmic disruption.

In considering the prophetic implications of the end times, the reappearance of "Nephilim-like" characteristics or influences suggests that humanity might once again grapple with challenges that obscure the lines between the spiritual and physical realms.

By understanding these ancient beings as an archetype, we're eager to delve deeper into the multifaceted fabric of eschatology. It allows us to see beyond the surface, anticipate and recognize patterns, and understand that the past often holds the keys to deciphering the future.

Supernatural Entities in the End Times

The Book of Revelation and other apocalyptic writings teem with descriptions of supernatural beings: beasts, dragons, and a horde of otherworldly creatures. The Book of Revelation and other eschatological texts paint a vivid and often unsettling picture of the end times. These scriptures abound with ethereal and fantastical creatures, including beasts with multi-headed forms, ferocious dragons, and armies of celestial entities. These depictions, undoubtedly, serve more than just a symbolic or metaphorical purpose; they signify real entities, albeit existing in spiritual dimensions.

Though not overt, the connection to the Nephilim presents an intriguing possibility. As Genesis describes, the Nephilim were a hybrid offspring of the "sons of God" and the "daughters of men," showcasing an unnatural confluence of the heavenly and the earthly. Similarly, the beings depicted in apocalyptic writings could represent a synthesis of realms, perhaps a fusion of spiritual entities with terrestrial elements, bringing about beings of immense power and authority.

This confluence of realms is not merely an incidental overlap; it underscores the essence of the end times—a period marked by the thinning veil between the physical and the spiritual. Like the Nephilim of ancient times, these beings might possess capabilities beyond human comprehension, enabling them to wield considerable influence over both the spiritual and physical dimensions.

More importantly, the adversarial nature of these entities aligns with the Nephilim's ancient narrative. Just as the Nephilim were said to challenge God's design and disrupt the moral fabric of early human societies, these end-times creatures seem poised to oppose God's redemptive plan for humanity, manifesting as spiritual tormentors and physical adversaries.

In navigating the eschatological future, understanding these supernatural entities' nature, purpose, and tactics becomes paramount. Their presence reinforces the gravity of the cosmic conflict between good and evil, urging believers to be equipped, vigilant, and rooted in the foundational truths of their faith.

Challenging Divine Authority

The Nephilim aberration served not only as a grievous insult to the Creator but also acted as a precursor to the gravity of rebellions to come. Fast-forward to prophetic scriptures, and one observes potent parallels in figures like the Antichrist and the Beast from the sea. The Antichrist mainly embodies this rebellion against divine authority. By setting himself up as God, he doesn't merely challenge God's sovereignty—he audaciously attempts to usurp it, echoing the hubris that the Nephilim once embodied.

The Beast, too, draws authority from the dragon, which is symbolic of Satan, further emphasizing the alignment of these end-time entities with forces that diametrically oppose God's design and will. This alignment is not just a mere repetition of past offenses but represents an amplification—a culmination of sorts—of the various challenges to divine sovereignty scattered throughout biblical history.

In drawing these connections between the Nephilim and end-time figures, it becomes clear that the Bible continually warns against the dangers of entities and forces that seek to disrupt the established order. These cautionary tales, both from the ancient past and prophetic future, underscore the enduring nature of the cosmic battle between good and evil and the consistent attempts to challenge divine preeminence.

God's People Amidst Chaos

In the pages of biblical history, the epoch of the Nephilim stands as a poignant reminder of humanity's capacity for wickedness, yet juxtaposed against this dark backdrop was the unwavering faith of Noah. An exemplar of righteousness, Noah's unwavering devotion provided a glimmer of hope amidst an era steeped in iniquity. This narrative arc, resonating with themes of faith amidst adversity, will find echoes in the end times.

Much like the days of old, the final chapter of human history will be tinged with overwhelming darkness. As Nephilim-like entities emerge, wielding their unprecedented powers and influencing societies, moral compasses will be skewed, and spiritual landscapes will be treacherous. Yet, just as the darkness seemed all-consuming during Noah's time, a faithful remnant will rise again.

Much like Noah, these stalwart believers will be distinguished not by their numbers but by the luminosity of their faith. They will remain undeterred in a world susceptible to deception and ensnared by supernatural entanglements, holding fast to the sacred scriptures and divine revelations. Their lives will be sanctuaries of purity, contrasting starkly with the surrounding moral decay.

Moreover, this remnant will not be mere passive observers. Called to be torchbearers of God's enduring truth, they will shine as beacons, guiding lost souls through the tumultuous waters of the end times. Their testimonies, underscored by unwavering trust in God's promises, will serve as lifelines for many, drawing them out of darkness and into the marvelous light of redemption.

While the end times will rekindle ancient challenges, invoking memories of the Nephilim era, it will resurrect old hopes. Just as Noah's ark stood as a symbol of salvation amidst judgment, the faithful remnant of the last days will be living testimonies of God's unfailing love and redemptive plan for humanity.

While shrouded in mystery, the Nephilim provides an essential lens to discern potential patterns in the end times. As we revisit this archetype, it's crucial to remember that understanding these patterns isn't about fear but preparedness. Awareness of the cosmic disruptions and challenges allows believers to remain rooted in faith, drawing strength from God's promise of ultimate victory over all forms of chaos and rebellion.

Unveiling Deception: The Subtle Seductions of the End Times

Understanding the depth of the spiritual landscape requires a grasp of historical and cultural nuances. The ancient Near Eastern contexts, which have left indelible marks on biblical texts, are essential to unlocking these nuances. As we dive into these texts, we discover a pattern: many cunning tactics forewarned for the end times are not new but refinements of age-old strategies.

From the Garden of Eden to the courts of Pharaoh, history is replete with examples of spiritual deception that have ensnared individuals and entire nations. These episodes, when viewed through the lens of the ancient Near East, provide a roadmap to discern the evolving tactics of spiritual adversaries. By studying these patterns, believers can better prepare themselves for the unique challenges of the end times.

The end times, as foretold, will be an era marked by heightened spiritual warfare. However, instead of overt confrontations, the emphasis will be on subtle seductions—deceptions that lure individuals away from divine truths. These may manifest in the form of distorted teachings, false prophets, or alluring ideologies that deviate from the core tenets of faith.

But with awareness comes empowerment. By recognizing these age-old tactics and understanding their roots, believers can fortify themselves against them. The challenge lies in resisting these deceptions and actively promoting and safeguarding the unadulterated truths of the faith. As the spiritual landscape of the world grows ever more complex, an informed and discerning approach will be the believer's most potent weapon.

Fortifying Faith Against Age-Old Deceptions

1. The Nature of Deception

Deception, especially as depicted in biblical contexts, is a profoundly intricate ploy. It goes beyond the simplicity of direct falsehoods, venturing into the treacherous territory of half-truths and misleading portrayals. These deceptions, particularly those forewarned in the context of end times, are designed to mirror truth closely enough to trap even those well-versed in their faith. Jesus, in Matthew 24:24, warned of false prophets and messiahs performing great signs and wonders, with the potential to deceive even the chosen ones if possible. This warning underscores the gravity of end-time deception. It isn't about outright fabrications but rather the insidious manipulation of divine truths, reshaping them just enough to seem plausible. As the end times approach, believers must be equipped with discernment, understanding that the most compelling lies are often masked in a cloak of familiarity, bearing semblance to the truth they've always known.

2. The Re-emergence of Ancient Pagan Practices

Throughout history, the ancient Near Eastern religions have venerated many deities, each associated with specific aspects of life, nature, or cosmic phenomena. Though seemingly archaic, these practices held deep cultural significance and shaped the beliefs, rituals, and daily lives of ancient societies. As we progress into the end times, it's conceivable that the allure of these ancient spiritualities might experience a revival.

Given our world's modern sensibilities, this re-emergence might not manifest explicitly as the age-old worship of ancient gods. Instead, they could be subtly interwoven into contemporary spiritual practices, packaged as new-age enlightenment or alternative pathways to spirituality. Though cloaked in the guise of progressiveness and inclusivity, these modern iterations might retain their core opposition to monotheistic beliefs.

The challenge for believers in such times would be discerning the origins and implications of these spiritual trends, ensuring they remain steadfast in their commitment to worshiping the one true God. The evolving landscape of spirituality requires a deep understanding of one's faith and the wisdom to distinguish between genuine spiritual growth and the snares of ancient deceptions refurbished for a new age.

3. The Supernatural as the Norm

The concept of a tangible spiritual realm, as opposed to a purely metaphorical one, has profound implications for our understanding of reality. Intertwined with ours, this realm plays a crucial role in the unfolding of cosmic events, especially as we approach the end times. The barriers separating the seen and unseen may grow thinner, making their interactions more pronounced and frequent.

In such a scenario, supernatural occurrences, including miracles, signs, and wonders, would not be rare but might become the order of the day. Yet, it's vital to recognize that the source of these marvels won't solely be divine. False prophets and the Antichrist, possessing powers granted by darker entities, will also perform feats that can deceive many. They would intend to mislead and captivate the masses, using these wonders as validations of their false teachings.

Hence, for believers, the actual test is not acknowledging the miracle but discerning its origin and intent. It necessitates a grounded understanding of one's faith and a commitment to divine principles. Every supernatural occurrence will need to be weighed against the teachings of the Scripture. The allegiance and message behind each wonder will be the definitive markers of its authenticity, reminding believers that not all that glitters, even in the spiritual realm, is gold.

4. Syncretism and Spiritual Pluralism

Syncretism, at its core, is a merging of disparate religious doctrines, rituals, and practices. While this may seem like a noble endeavor, promoting unity and coexistence, its ramifications could be far-reaching, especially in the context of end-times prophecies. The allure of such a movement would be undeniable. In a world fraught with religious conflicts and divisions, the idea of a unified global faith might appear as the panacea for humanity's spiritual and social ailments.

This new-world faith would likely emphasize commonalities, minimizing differences to forge a sense of unity. Sacred texts might be reinterpreted or amalgamated, creating a universally palatable doctrine. Rituals, too, might see a fusion, combining elements from various faith traditions to form a unique and eclectic blend of worship. On the surface, this would present a utopian vision: a world where religious discord is a thing of the past, replaced by mutual respect and collective worship.

However, this blending poses a significant threat to Christianity, which holds specific truths about God, salvation, and the nature of reality. Christianity's fundamental tenets, like the deity of Christ, His resurrection, and the path to salvation through Him, contrast sharply with many other religious beliefs. By diluting or compromising these doctrines for the sake of unity, the very essence of the Christian faith would be at risk.

The push for a global religion might be presented under the guise of tolerance, inclusivity, and peace, making it a compelling proposition for many. But beneath the surface, it's a strategic move to neutralize the transformative power of genuine faith. For believers, the challenge would be to discern between honest interfaith dialogue—which respects and understands differences—and syncretistic efforts that threaten to erode the foundational truths of their faith.

5. Redefining Morality

The trajectory of societal morality has always been fluid, influenced by cultural, political, and philosophical shifts. In the context of the end times, this fluidity might reach unprecedented extremes. What was once on society's fringes might center-stage, redefining the core of what is deemed acceptable or "normal." This metamorphosis will not merely be a matter of evolving social conventions. Still, it might be presented as progressive enlightenment, a shedding of "archaic" values in favor of a new, liberated moral order.

Technological advancements and their profound influence on societal norms could play a pivotal role in this shift. Integrating artificial intelligence, biotechnology, and virtual realities might challenge our understanding of human nature, identity, and relationships. Ethical dilemmas arising from these advancements could further blur the lines of biblical morality

Furthermore, global interconnectedness, facilitated by the internet and social media, could lead to a homogenization of moral values. Once insulated and distinct, local cultural norms might be swayed by dominant global narratives. Often framed in the language of human rights, inclusivity, and personal freedom, these narratives could wield powerful influence, making any dissenting voice seem regressive or even harmful.

The challenge will be multifold for those who hold steadfast to biblical principles. Not only will they grapple with the internal conflict of navigating a world that increasingly contradicts their beliefs, but they may also face external pressures. This could range from subtle social ostracization to more overt forms of discrimination or even persecution. In such a climate, maintaining one's faith would require personal conviction and communal support. Churches and faith communities would become essential bastions of hope, encouragement, and resistance, reminding believers of timeless truths amidst rapidly changing mores.

6. Doubting Divine Providence

The subversion of trust in God's sovereignty is a foundational tactic, as it attempts to dislodge the very anchor of a believer's faith. The fabric of a believer's relationship with the divine is strained by suggesting that God is not wholly in control or that His intentions might not be benevolent. This erosion of trust can have cascading effects, leading to confusion, disillusionment, and a weakened resolve to follow God's directives.

Modern manifestations of this strategy could be multifaceted. For one, there might be a rise in philosophies or spiritual teachings that emphasize a human-centric universe, pushing the narrative that humanity is the ultimate authority and has no overarching divine plan. Such beliefs can be seductive, as they appeal to human pride and the desire for autonomy. By placing humans at the center of the universe, the need for divine guidance or intervention seems redundant.

Additionally, there may be a proliferation of media content—be it films, books, or online narratives—that subtly mocks or questions God's nature. These could depict Him as a fallible being, prone to mistakes or whimsical decisions. Alternatively, God could be represented as cold and impersonal, a force that sets the universe into motion but remains indifferent to individual lives and struggles.

Scientific or philosophical discourses might further compound this by suggesting that everything can be explained without invoking a higher power. The marvels of the universe, the intricacies of life, and even human consciousness might be reduced to mere products of chance and natural processes.

In such an environment, believers would need to root themselves deeply in personal experiences with God and rely on the time-tested wisdom of Scripture. A vibrant personal relationship with God, fortified through prayer, worship, and community, can be a bulwark against these insidious doubts. In this way, believers can reaffirm the timeless truth that God is both sovereign and intimately involved in the details of their lives, guiding, providing for, and loving them unconditionally.

7. *The Allure of Forbidden Knowledge*

The allure of forbidden knowledge has been a recurring theme throughout human history, often rooted in the desire for empowerment, transcendence, or a deeper understanding of existence. From the early narratives of Eden, where the promise of being "like God" was the bait to the various secret societies and esoteric orders throughout history, the appeal of hidden wisdom has never truly waned.

In the end times, this fascination could take on heightened proportions. With the advancements in technology and communication, accessing and spreading these alternative teachings and practices will be more accessible than ever before. Virtual realities, augmented experiences, and interactive platforms might be used to immerse individuals in ancient rituals or to access what is perceived as arcane wisdom.

There could also be a resurgence of ancient mystical traditions. Neo-paganism, sorcery, and the likes might experience a revival, not as mere curiosities, but as viable spiritual paths. The increasing skepticism and disillusionment with established religious institutions might drive many to explore these alternative avenues.

The danger, however, is that these practices, while seemingly enlightening, can divert seekers from the simplicity and purity of faith in God. They might promote a self-centric approach to spirituality, emphasizing self-divination, self-godhood, or achieving power and knowledge at any cost.

Furthermore, the end times might witness an increase in purported spiritual experiences—visions, prophecies, and signs from beings or forces outside the realm of traditional Judeo-Christian understanding. These might be so convincing in their authenticity that even some devout believers could be led astray.

In such a charged atmosphere, believers must root their faith in the foundational truths of Scripture and maintain a close relationship with God. This relationship should be nurtured through consistent prayer, fellowship, and grounding in the Word. While the mysteries of the universe can be enticing, it's essential to remember that true wisdom and power come from a relationship with God and not from the fleeting allure of forbidden knowledge.

Stand for Truth

The intricacies of end-time deceptions will not necessarily present as blatant challenges but as nuanced allurements, gradually steering individuals from God's unfailing truth. Such tactics have been witnessed since ancient times, underscoring believers' need to be discerning and firmly rooted in the Scriptures. The actual test lies not merely in identifying the false but in tenaciously clinging to the truth amidst a world growing more adversarial towards it.

Redefining Morality: A Closer Examination

The evolving nature of morality has consistently been a focal point of debate, spanning both religious and secular spheres. Delving into ancient contexts reveals the historical fluidity of moral values, providing insights into their potential trajectories in end-time scenarios.

Historical Roots

Throughout history, moral values have often been intertwined with societal norms, cultural practices, and religious beliefs. In the ancient world, for example:

- **Empire Expansion and Cultural Absorption:** As empires like the Romans or Babylonians expanded, they encountered many cultural practices and beliefs. Often, they integrated these practices into their societal fabric. What might have been taboo or immoral in one culture could become normalized in another due to political or societal pressures.

- **Religious Rituals:** Ancient religions had rituals and practices that might seem abhorrent to modern sensibilities, from human sacrifices to ritual prostitution. These were considered morally acceptable within their cultural and religious frameworks, emphasizing the relative nature of morality in different epochs.

Modern Manifestation

Today, morality is at a significant crossroads due to various factors:

- **Technological Advancements:** Innovations, especially in bioethics, genetics, and artificial intelligence, challenge traditional moral paradigms. Questions about cloning, genetic modification, AI rights, and technology integration into human biology make us reconsider what it means to be human and what boundaries we're willing to cross.

- ***Cultural Relativism:*** As global communication shrinks, there's a growing acceptance of the idea that morality is culturally relative—that there's no absolute moral truth, but rather various truths shaped by cultural experiences.

- ***Personal Autonomy:*** Individualism, especially in Western cultures, has led to the belief that personal freedom and autonomy are paramount. This often results in a "live and let live" attitude, where anything that doesn't harm another person is considered morally acceptable.

- ***Legal Shifts:*** Laws, which are often a reflection of societal moral standards, are changing rapidly. Issues like drug use, sexuality, euthanasia, and freedom of speech are seeing legal shifts that reflect evolving societal values, sometimes conflicting with traditional religious beliefs.

End Times Implications

The prophetic literature, especially in the New Testament, suggests that the end times will be characterized by a form of godlessness (2 Timothy 3:1-This doesn't necessarily imply atheism but rather a rejection of traditional, God-centered moral values. If we extrapolate from current trends:

- ***Normalized Immorality:*** Practices once considered immoral by biblical standards might not only be accepted but also celebrated. The delineation between good and evil might be obscured, with moral judgments based on societal consensus rather than absolute standards.

- ***Persecution:*** Those adhering to biblical moral standards might be marginalized, ridiculed, or even persecuted. As society moves further from these standards, biblical beliefs might be considered outdated, biased, or harmful.

The fluidity of morality, especially in the context of the end times, isn't just a theological or philosophical concern. It's a pressing, practical issue for believers navigating a world where the moral goalposts continually shift. Grounding oneself in Scripture, understanding the historical roots of moral shifts, and engaging in compassionate dialogue are essential for Christians aiming to live out their faith authentically in such times.

The enigmatic tale of the Nephilim and the intricate cosmic scenarios from the days of Noah provides a profound reflection on the challenge's humanity has faced when confronted with beings that blur the boundaries between the divine and the human. As we close this illuminating chapter, we understand more deeply the timeless struggle between humanity's aspirations and religious order. This tension becomes even more palpable as we transition into our next chapter on Transhumanism. Here, we will delve into the modern quest for human enhancement and the age-old desire to transcend our natural limitations—a pursuit reminiscent of humanity's aspiration to be like God. The parallels between these ancient and futuristic epochs invite us to contemplate deeply about our place in the universe and our relationship with the Divine.

Chapter 7

Transhumanism, Technology, and the God-Man in The End Times

> *Then they said, "Come, let us build ourselves a city and a tower with its top in the heavens, and let us make a name for ourselves, lest we be dispersed over the face of the whole earth." (Genesis 11:4)*

Transhumanism, while promising breakthroughs that could dramatically extend life, enhance our cognitive and physical abilities, and even transcend biological boundaries, is not just a scientific endeavor; it's also a philosophical and spiritual frontier. The push to enhance and possibly exceed human limits has roots in the age-old human desire to become like gods—a theme that echoes back to the earliest biblical narratives, such as the account of Adam and Eve in the Garden of Eden. The allure of obtaining godlike knowledge and abilities is not new; what is novel is the avenue through which humanity now seeks this elevation. In these advancements, there arises a pressing need for discernment. As we inch closer to achieving these godlike capacities, we must reflect on their ramifications for our bodies and societies and our souls. How do these aspirations align with or diverge from god's design and intention for humanity? The subsequent exploration will dive deeper into these questions, unveiling the interplay between the aspirations of transhumanism and the timeless truths of scripture.

Transhumanism's promise: Utopia or dystopia? A deeper delve

The allure of transhumanism is undeniable. Picture a world where Alzheimer's is a thing of the past; amputees regain full function through biomechanically perfect limbs, or virtual realities are so rich and immersive that they rival or surpass our physical existence. Such a world seems like the next logical step in our evolutionary journey, a testament to human ingenuity and resilience.

However, beneath the surface of these advancements lies a series of profound philosophical, ethical, and spiritual questions. If we can extend our lifespan indefinitely, what does that mean for our understanding of life's value or purpose? If we can enhance our cognitive abilities, where do we draw the line between organic human consciousness and an artificially augmented one? And as we merge more with machines or digital avatars, what becomes of the human soul?

Furthermore, the accessibility of such technologies raises concerns about societal inequalities. Will these advancements be available to all, or will they widen the gap between the haves and the have-nots, leading to a new class of superhumans versus the rest?

In essence, while transhumanism promises a future teeming with unparalleled potential, it also beckons us to tread cautiously. As history has shown, not all that glitters are gold. As we stand on the cusp of potentially redefining humanity, it becomes imperative to not only marvel at our technological prowess but also deeply ponder the essence of what it means to be human and the values that should guide our journey forward.

The utopian dream: humanity's age-old quest

Transhumanism, in its modern guise, simply channels this perennial aspiration through the prism of cutting-edge technology and science. At its core, it's a story as old as time: the human spirit, indefatigable and ever-curious, seeking to break the chains of its earthly confines and ascend to greater heights.

Throughout history, our species has showcased an unyielding drive to surpass boundaries. Ancient civilizations, from the Egyptians with their intricate mummification processes to the Greeks with their pantheon of gods and demigods, have all grappled with the constraints of mortality and the dream of transcending them. Myths and legends from every corner of the globe speak of heroes embarking on dangerous quests to acquire knowledge, power, or the secret to eternal life.

Alchemy, once deemed a precursor to modern chemistry, was rooted in the desire to transform base metals into gold, but more profoundly, it pursued the elixir of life. This substance would confer youth and longevity. Similarly, religions and spiritual paths worldwide offer visions of afterlives, reincarnations, or states of enlightenment where the human soul transcends the cycle of birth and death.

In this context, transhumanism emerges as the latest chapter in this grand saga. With biotechnology, nanotechnology, and artificial intelligence as its tools, it aims to realize what was once deemed the domain of gods or the stuff of myths. However, the ethical problems it presents are unparalleled. While the ancients sought divine intervention or mystic artifacts, today's pursuit is intertwined with complex moral quandaries about the very essence of our being. The journey, fraught with both promise and peril, beckons us to reflect deeply on our place in the universe and the nature of the legacy we wish to create.

Modern transhumanism translates these ancient dreams into the language of science and technology:

Overcoming disease: Genetic engineering promises to eradicate hereditary diseases and potentially enhance physical and cognitive abilities.

Augmented reality and enhanced cognition: Brain-computer interfaces, such as Elon Musk's neural link, could usher in a new era of human understanding, where knowledge is instantaneously accessible.

Eternal life: The ultimate transhumanist goal, arguably, is to conquer death, either through biological means or by transferring human consciousness into machines or virtual realities.

The dystopian shadow: potential pitfalls and ethical quandaries

While the promises above are undeniably compelling, they cast a long, often troubling shadow:

Playing god: Just as the builders of Babel sought to "make a name for themselves" (Genesis 11:4), transhumanism treads the fine line of overreach. By seeking to control and modify the essence of human life, we enter territory traditionally ascribed to the divine. Our exploration of religious boundaries in the biblical narrative underscores the dangers of such overreach.

Social inequities: Transhumanist technologies might not be accessible to all, potentially leading to a society where the enhanced and the unenhanced live in starkly different realities. This could exacerbate existing social hierarchies and inequalities, leading to a new class system based on biological or cognitive enhancement.

Loss of humanity: In seeking to transcend our limitations, there's a genuine risk of losing what makes us inherently human. Emotions, imperfections, and the very experience of life could be altered irreversibly, leading to profound existential and philosophical crises.

Unintended consequences: From a purely pragmatic standpoint, the modifications proposed by transhumanists could have unforeseen side effects. Genetic changes could lead to new diseases or biological problems. Merging human cognition with AI might lead to unexpected psychological or neurological issues.

A biblical perspective

Transhumanism mirrors humanity's timeless tug-of-war between divine purpose and personal ambition. While scripture celebrates the pursuit of knowledge and enlightenment, it simultaneously offers cautionary tales of unchecked human endeavors that bypass godly counsel. The allure of transhumanism, with its glittering vision of an augmented future, demands careful consideration. As we edge closer to these transformative shifts, it's crucial to balance the promises of a utopian imagination with the risks of unintended consequences while anchored in timeless ethical values.

The march of technology is relentless and, in many ways, awe-inspiring. Each invention has transformed societies and reshaped human experiences from the wheel to the World Wide Web. Yet, as we stand at the cusp of even more groundbreaking innovations, it's evident that technology's influence isn't unilaterally positive. Weaving together ancient texts and modern insights, we can understand technology's duality more profoundly.

Throughout history, technological advancements, from the invention of the printing press to the dawn of the internet, have expanded access to information and amplified individual voices. These innovations can challenge traditional power structures and pave the way for a more equitable distribution of knowledge and influence.

Medical innovations continually redefine the boundaries of healing. With tools ranging from life-enhancing prosthetics to the groundbreaking capabilities of CRISPR, technology paves the path toward a world with reduced pain and suffering. Moreover, inventions like the internet have woven societies into a closely-knit global fabric. The vast expanse of geographical space seems trivial when set against the backdrop of our interconnected digital realm, promoting a sense of worldwide unity and collective consciousness.

The cutting edge: the perils of technology

However, the very technologies that promise utopia can also create dystopia:

Connectivity versus loneliness: The rise of technology, while fostering global connectivity, can inadvertently heighten feelings of solitude and disconnection. As the digital realm becomes increasingly influential, the authenticity of human relationships risks being overshadowed by fleeting online engagements. Mental health issues may amplify due to this virtual preference, and the depth and richness of face-to-face relationships might be jeopardized.

Ethical complexity in biotechnologies: The advancements in biotechnologies, especially in arenas like genetic engineering, place us at the crossroads of innovation and ethical dilemmas. While the potential to edit genes and combat diseases is awe-inspiring, its ushers in many questions. For instance, beyond addressing health issues, is it ethical to modify genes to augment intelligence or beauty? At what juncture do we transition from therapeutic interventions to overstepping our natural boundaries?

Digital oversight and privacy concerns: As we navigate the digital epoch, we're graced with convenience but also confronted with invasive surveillance mechanisms. Each online interaction, whether a click, share, or comment, leaves an indelible digital imprint. These breadcrumbs can be aggregated, scrutinized, and occasionally exploited, posing dire threats to individual privacy and civil liberties.

Economic transitions and disruptions: The advent of avant-garde technologies, notably in artificial intelligence and robotics, foreshadows potential upheavals in traditional work spheres. While these shifts will usher in innovative job roles and opportunities, the intervening period might be fraught with challenges, exacerbating economic divides and stoking societal tensions.

Biblical echoes and insights

The tale of the Tower of Babel in Genesis provides a profound reflection on the perils of unchecked ambition and humanity's propensity to overreach. The audacious attempt to erect a structure reaching the heavens was not merely an architectural marvel but an emblem of human defiance and self-reliance, overshadowing divine purpose. In today's era, our cutting-edge technological exploits resonate with this narrative, illustrating the perennial tension between human aspiration and the designs of the sacred.

As custodians of creation, the bible implores us to exercise wisdom and thoughtful stewardship (Genesis 1:28; Proverbs 3:13-18). In this light, our technological pursuits demand introspection and discernment. These endeavors, while transformative, must be balanced with an acute awareness of their broader implications on the spiritual, moral, and ethical fabric of society.

Furthermore, biblical admonitions against idolatry extend beyond the mere adoration of carved figures or sacred edifices. Idolatry can manifest in myriad forms, with its core being an undue reverence for anything that challenges the importance of the divine. In our contemporary setting, where technology is deeply intertwined with daily existence, the peril lies in elevating it to a pedestal, mistaking its profound capacities for promises of ultimate salvation. This calls for a recalibration of our perspectives, ensuring that our faith in technology remains anchored in humility and recognizing its limits.

The narrative of the Tower of Babel encapsulated in Genesis, paints a vivid portrait of humanity's tendency towards arrogance and pride. This monumental attempt to craft a skyscraping tower reaching the heavens symbolizes more than just an architectural feat; it represents human audacity, a rebellion against divine order in pursuit of autonomy. The Tower of Babel is an emblematic tale, presaging a recurring motif across ages: the delicate interplay between human ambition and divine blueprint.

In our current age, this narrative is reinvigorated with striking intensity as we stand at the threshold of what might be termed the "homo deus" era. This term, implying "god-like humans," encapsulates a vision of humanity transformed by its technological prowess. As biotechnologies, artificial intelligence, and other advanced fields offer promises of transcending biological limitations, the homo deus vision nudges humanity closer to the aspiration of godhood.

However, akin to the tower of Babel, the ascent towards homo Deus is laden with profound ethical dilemmas and existential inquiries. Are we, once again, challenging the boundaries set by the divine? While the bible encourages wisdom and thoughtful stewardship in our dominion over creation (Genesis 1:28; Proverbs 3:13-18), it also serves as a compass, warning against the pitfalls of unchecked ambition.

Biblical warnings against idolatry, while historically contextualized by statues and temples, bear a universal truth. When placed on a pedestal that challenges the sanctity of the divine, anything morphs into an idol. Today, as the allure of technology and the dream of homo deus beckon, there's a lurking danger: the deification of human achievement. We are mistaking our tools and advancements as definitive solutions that can lead to a modern form of idolatry, where technology and the dream of homo deus overshadow the divine's central place in the human.

End times prophecies: echoes of deception

The New Testament contains several references to deceptions in the end times. In his letters, Paul warns of a great falling away and the mystery of lawlessness (2 Thessalonians 2:3-7). While it's speculative to tie these directly to transhumanism, the parallels are worth noting. Transhumanism's allure is rooted in humanity's control over its destiny, potentially sidelining god's sovereignty. The figure of the antichrist, delineated in sacred scriptures, symbolizes the pinnacle of human defiance against god. It's feasible that a world embracing transhumanist ideals would be fertile ground for such a figure to emerge, promising an artificial utopia.

As depicted in various scriptures, the end times signify the zenith of an ancient struggle between divine truths and human distortions. As we approach this pinnacle, the nature of deception becomes increasingly insidious. Rather than overt deviations from the truth, these deceptions present themselves as subtle twists so craftily interwoven that even those deeply rooted in faith might be tempted to waver. This is a caution mirrored in the words of Jesus, where he warns of false prophets performing great signs and wonders, potent enough to mislead even the chosen ones (Matthew 24:24). Within this backdrop, the melding of transhumanism and technology offers a compelling narrative. As humanity strives for godlike powers and knowledge, potentially reaching the era of "homo deus," this ambition might be perceived as the culmination of human progress. Yet, from a scriptural perspective, it also raises profound questions. In our pursuit of transcendence, are we inadvertently setting the stage for the great delusion prophesied in ancient texts? The journey to decipher truth from deceit requires astute spiritual discernment, especially as the boundaries between man and machine, natural and supernatural, begin to blur.

Homo deus: dangers and deceptions in the age of divine man

The Latin term "homo deus," translating to "god-man," encapsulates the lofty ambitions of the transhumanist movement. It paints a vision where humans ascend to a godlike status through the integration of advanced technologies, transcending our biological limitations. The idea is popularized in modern culture, notably through works like yuval Noah Harari's book "homo deus." but, when examined in the light of biblical texts, one realizes that the concept may not be as novel or as helpful as it first appears.

The concept of homo deus

The concept of homo deus is not merely the next step in human evolution but a radical departure from the natural trajectory of humanity as we know it. This vision embodies the fusion of our biological essence with the might of technology, birthing a species that marries the organic with the synthetic. The driving force behind this ambition is the age-old human desire for perfection, longevity, and omnipotence.

Envision a world where the frailties that define the human experience—our susceptibility to diseases, our mental limitations, our emotional vulnerabilities—are things of the past. With technology acting as the catalyst, this homo Deus would not just be free from the vulnerabilities that have plagued humanity since its inception but wield powers reminiscent of deities from ancient mythologies. Bioengineered bodies could regenerate, neural interfaces could expand cognitive functions to unimaginable horizons, and our very consciousness might even find new homes beyond the biological, perhaps in virtual realms or silicon-based architectures.

This paradigm also challenges our core understanding of values, purpose, and spirituality. If suffering and the inevitability of death are eradicated, what becomes human, resilience and spirit? Moreover, as humans come close to achieving a god-like status, it beckons more profound existential questions: What does it mean to be human when the limitations that have defined our species no longer apply? And, in our relentless pursuit of divinity, do we risk losing the very essence that makes us human?

The dream of homo deus, while tantalizing with its promises, also casts a long shadow of ethical dilemmas, philosophical quandaries, and spiritual problems. In our journey to transcend mortality and imperfection, we are not just reshaping our future but are also, inadvertently, redrafting the very fabric of our identity.

Potential dangers and deceptions

The *illusion of self-salvation*

With its ambitious agenda of surpassing human limitations through technology and innovation, Transhumanism offers a vision of salvation rooted in human achievement. It beckons with the allure of a future where our inherent vulnerabilities are no longer an impediment, where science and technology act as saviors, liberating us from the chains of mortality, cognitive constraints, and physical frailties. The core proposition is that with enough time, effort, and ingenuity, humanity can craft its destiny, free from the imperfections that have long defined our existence.

This notion starkly contrasts the biblical narrative, where salvation is not something humans can attain through their own merits, no matter how noble or groundbreaking. Instead, it's a divine gift, an act of grace from a benevolent creator who seeks a relationship with his creation. In this spiritual framework, salvation is more than just physical or cognitive emancipation—it's a holistic reconciliation of humanity with god, encompassing spiritual, emotional, and relational dimensions.

The potential pitfall of the transhumanist vision is that it places an immense burden on human shoulders. It instills the belief that we are the sole architects of our destiny, and any failure to realize this techno-utopian dream reflects a deficit in our innovation or willpower. This can lead to a cycle of perpetual striving, with humanity always on the lookout for the next technological fix, upgrade, and leap that promises to bring us closer to that ideal.

Furthermore, we risk inflating the human ego and pride by leaning heavily into our capabilities and sidelining the divine. The ancient warning of hubris rings true here. The outcome can be unpredictable when humans see themselves as the sole custodians of their fate, unchecked by any higher moral or spiritual authority.

Ultimately, while Transhumanism's aspirations aren't inherently nefarious, and many of its goals, such as alleviating suffering and disease, are commendable, it's crucial to approach such a powerful ideology with discernment. As we stand at the crossroads of unprecedented technological advancements, the age-old wisdom of understanding our place in the grand tapestry of existence and recognizing the limits of human endeavor becomes ever more relevant.

Redefining the imago dei

The belief that humanity is created in the image of god, the "imago dei," is a cornerstone of judeo-Christian thought. This concept isn't just about physical appearance but encompasses deeper facets such as moral reasoning, self-awareness, and the capacity for relational love. It implies a sacredness and intrinsic worth to every human life, establishing a direct connection between the creator and the created. Being made in god's image endows us with responsibilities and a sense of purpose; it reminds us of our divine origin and eternal destiny.

Enter the realm of transhumanism, which encourages technological interventions to enhance human capabilities. On the surface, these enhancements might seem purely beneficial, aimed at eliminating diseases, prolonging life, or augmenting cognitive abilities. However, a deeper introspection raises critical questions: At what point do these enhancements alter the essence of what it means to be human? If we modify our genetic code, integrate our brains with machines, or attain digital immortality, are we still reflecting the image of god, or are we entering uncharted territories, rewriting the fundamental code of our being?

This transition could usher in profound theological dilemmas. For instance, if our cognition is enhanced to superhuman levels, how does that affect our moral and ethical decision-making? If we can artificially prolong life, how does that influence our understanding of mortality, soul, and the afterlife? Moreover, where does the divine spark reside if our essence becomes a blend of organic and inorganic?

Existential crises might also arise. An individual, augmented to the point of being beyond human, might grapple with questions of identity, purpose, and belonging. Such individuals might feel isolated, struggling to find their place in a society that might view them with awe, envy, or fear.

While technological advancements in transhumanism hold promise, they also present challenges that strike at the core of our understanding of humanity's place in the divine order. It's a journey fraught with ethical, theological, and existential challenges that require deep contemplation and discernment.

Moral and ethical dilemmas

The accelerating march of technology has continuously redefined the realms of possibility. With each breakthrough, boundaries once thought insurmountable are pushed further, presenting a tantalizing horizon of potential. However, this relentless progression, while awe-inspiring, brings a multitude of ethical dilemmas that challenge our fundamental understanding of right and wrong.

Consider genetic editing. Techniques such as CRISPR offer the tantalizing promise of eradicating genetic disorders and diseases. Yet, the same tools that can prevent hereditary illnesses might also be used to engineer 'designer babies', leading to eugenics-like practices where certain traits, perhaps even extending to cognitive abilities or physical appearance, are favored over others. This not only presents medical risks but raises profound moral questions. What are the implications of such a society, where the very essence of a human can be selected or discarded based on societal standards?

Similarly, the fusion of AI and human cognition, while offering enhancements in memory, intelligence, or even sensory perception, begs the question: at what point does the human being end and the machine begin? Such augmentations might lead to an altered state of consciousness or even a revised definition of human identity. With blurred lines between man and machine, issues of rights, responsibilities, and personhood come to the fore.

The notion of "uploading" human consciousness is perhaps the most ethereal of these difficulties. It delves deep into philosophical debates about the nature of the soul, consciousness, and existence. If one's consciousness could exist independently of the body, what does being human mean? What is the nature of reality without sensory experiences or corporeal limitations? Moreover, who controls this digital realm? The potential for exploitation, manipulation, or even a form of "digital purgatory" becomes all too real.

These revolutionary capabilities highlight the urgency for a grounded ethical framework. Historically, humanity has often navigated the consequences of its innovations post-facto, reacting to unforeseen complications after they arise. But a proactive approach is essential, with higher stakes than ever. Without a well-defined moral compass— anchored in timeless principles and higher truths—there's a genuine risk that we may lose sight of the essence that defines our humanity in our quest to push boundaries. The challenge, therefore, is not merely technological but profoundly philosophical and spiritual: how do we harness the boundless potential of technology while preserving the sanctity and dignity of the human spirit?

Anchoring aspirations

Transhumanism, situated at the intersection of technology and philosophy, paints a picture of a future filled with promise and uncertainties. With its rich tapestry of narratives and teachings, the bible cautions us against the perils of exceeding divinely established limits and the potential pitfalls of investing absolute faith in human accomplishments. As we venture into this uncharted territory, grounding our aspirations in the ageless wisdom of scripture becomes essential.

Biblical precedents: echoes of ancient ambitions

The narrative of homo deus, which envisions a future where humans ascend to god-like status through technological and biological enhancements, bears striking parallels to several ancient biblical stories. Chief among them is the Tower of Babel account, where humans are united in their endeavor to build a tower reaching the heavens, an audacious act of challenging divine authority and asserting their autonomy. This attempt to ascend to a higher realm or status, bypassing divine intent, finds a modern echo in the aspirations of transhumanism.

Similarly, the Genesis account of the Nephilim speaks of beings that were the offspring of "the sons of god" and "the daughters of men." These Nephilim, often described as giants or mighty, were neither divine nor purely human. Their very existence challenged the natural order and represented a blurring of the boundaries set by the divine. In the contemporary context, as we teeter on the brink of creating enhanced or hybrid beings through genetic modifications and artificial intelligence integrations, we are arguably revisiting similar questions about the sanctity of the natural order and the limits of our ambitions.

Both these ancient stories serve as cautionary tales, warning of the potential dangers when human ambition is left unchecked or when we overstep our bounds. They offer profound insights into the perils of hubris and the consequences of challenging or attempting to redefine the natural or divine order. As we venture into a future where the line between human and god-like beings becomes increasingly blurred, these age-old narratives provide invaluable reflections on our actions' philosophical, ethical, and spiritual ramifications.

Dangers and deceptions of the homo deus vision explored

The concept of homo deus, blending humans with godlike capabilities achieved through technological advancement, may initially seem like a captivating progression of our species. However, a web of potential dangers and deceptions emerges as we delve deeper into its implications, particularly in light of biblical teachings and insights from scholars like Dr. Michael Heiser and Thomas Horn.

The transhumanist ascent and echoes of the past

Transhumanism's promise of melding human biology with technology holds the possibility of pushing us beyond our innate boundaries. The melding of machine and man aims to redefine our essence, crossing the lines between the natural and the enhanced. Historically, we've seen similar motifs of transcending the human condition. The biblical tales of the Nephilim, born from the union of the "sons of god" and the "daughters of men," showcase beings with extraordinary abilities and an elevated stature that distinguished them from mere mortals. These narratives portray an intermingling of the divine and human, producing revered and feared entities in some interpretations.

This brings forth a compelling question: Are our endeavors toward transhumanism a modern manifestation of this age-old impulse? Are we driven by a deep longing to recapture a lost grandeur or achieve an unprecedented apotheosis? As we boldly chart this unexplored frontier, it's vital to be grounded in introspection and a sense of responsibility. The tales of the Nephilim, as distant and mythological as they might seem, resonate with the timeless message: With great power comes great responsibility. It's a call not just for scientific and technological prudence but also for exploring our souls, urging us to consider what it truly means to be human in an age of gods and machines.

Puzzles and warnings from beyond

The story of the Nephilim offers a poignant reflection on the complexities of unchecked power and the consequences of divorcing our abilities from moral and ethical considerations. As these beings stood tall, not just in stature but also in influence and capability, they inadvertently (or perhaps intentionally) perpetuated an environment that was antithetical to the harmonious order envisioned by the divine.

In their wake, society was riddled with excesses, imbalances, and a blatant disregard for the sanctity and value of life. Intertwined with human communities, their existence spawned not an era of enlightenment or prosperity but rather a descent into chaos. The foundations of moral order and societal coherence started to crumble, leading to an epoch so tainted that a divine intervention became necessary to reset the cosmic balance.

Drawing parallels with the transhumanist movement, there's is a glaring reminder. The quest for enhancement, the drive to supersede our biological and cognitive confines, is not inherently problematic. The spirit with which we approach this quest determines its outcome. If driven by sheer hubris, unchecked ambition, or a disregard for the intrinsic value of natural life and order, we might inadvertently set the stage for a world where technology and advancements create more problems than they solve.

Moreover, as we integrate with machines, edit our genes, and possibly even alter our consciousness, we must constantly ask ourselves: at what cost? What facets of our humanity might we lose in the process? How do we ensure these advancements benefit society rather than creating a new elite class or exacerbating existing inequalities?

The story of the Nephilim, a chapter from a distant past, mirrors our present and potential future, urging us to tread with caution, wisdom, and an unwavering commitment to the collective good. It's a sobering reminder that mere capability, devoid of ethical anchoring, can lead to cataclysm.

Concluding thoughts

For all its enigma and controversy, the UFO phenomenon is not merely a fringe element relegated to conspiracy theories or sci-fi fandom. It presents a multifaceted challenge, spanning the realms of science, theology, and even geopolitics. Reports of unidentified aerial phenomena (up), backed by increasingly credible evidence and testimonials, ignite questions that rattle the very core of our understanding of reality.

Could these unidentified entities be external civilizations reaching out, or perhaps a manifestation of something even more complex? And where does artificial intelligence—a rapidly advancing frontier in its own right—fit into this mosaic? Might there be an AI nexus that ties together the terrestrial, extraterrestrial, and spiritual dimensions?

Among other religious and philosophical texts, the Bible warns of end-time deceptions, scenarios wherein humanity might be led astray by powerful forces or persuasive narratives. With the rise of artificial intelligence and its potential fusion with human consciousness, there lies the prospect of constructing realities so compelling that they blur the lines between the genuine and the fabricated.

The convergence of transhumanist goals, the mystery of UFOs, and the omnipresent shadow of AI-LED realities can be likened to a cosmic puzzle. While distinct in its nature, each piece might collectively provide insights into the more giant mosaic of existence and, more pressingly, our place and path within it.

This journey of comprehension is not just a pursuit of knowledge but also a quest for spiritual and moral clarity. As we embark on this next chapter, let us be guided not just by scientific rigor but also by a compass calibrated by ethical values, historical lessons, and a genuine desire to uplift, not just evolve, humanity.

Chapter 8

UFOs, End Times Deception, and the AI Nexus

"For now, we see in a mirror dimly, but then face to face. Now I know in part; then I shall know fully" (1 Corinthians 13:12)

From the dawn of civilization to the contemporary age, humanity has witnessed events and trends defying simplistic interpretations in the grand tapestry of existence. These phenomena are intriguing anomalies, challenging our perception of reality and urging us to look beyond the mundane.

One of the most enigmatic phenomena is the proliferation of UFO sightings and encounters. From ancient mural depictions to modern-day fighter pilot testimonies, unidentified aerial phenomena have continually teased our understanding, inviting skepticism and wonder. They function as cosmic riddles, nudging us to question the boundaries of our known universe and our place within it.

Parallel to this, ancient scriptures and prophecies have long alluded to a period of grand deception in the final chapters of human history. These end-times warnings echoed across various religious texts highlight an era where truth becomes obfuscated, where humanity might be led astray by allurements both terrestrial and possibly extraterrestrial.

Enter the realm of artificial intelligence—our testament to human ingenuity and perhaps our most profound attempt at playing creator. We must grapple with profound questions as AI advances, mimicking and sometimes surpassing human intelligence. Could these creations of code and silicon be the very instruments or facilitators of the prophesied deception? Might they bridge the terrestrial and the extraterrestrial, decoding the enigma of UFOs or even synergizing with them?

As these narratives converge, they hint at an underlying spiritual tapestry that binds them together. The ethereal dance between the known and the unknown, the human and the beyond-human, points towards an unfolding cosmic drama. We are not mere spectators in this drama but active participants, and our technological and spiritual decisions hold ramifications that may reverberate across dimensions.

In recognizing these connections, we are invited to not only marvel at our existence's mysteries but also approach them with discernment. In understanding how UFO encounters, end-times prophecies, and AI intersect, we might gain insights into the more profound spiritual currents that guide the course of human destiny.

Echoes of the cosmos: the Nephilim, UFOS, and humanity's search for meaning

Drawing parallels between ancient accounts of the Nephilim and contemporary UFO encounters is a fascinating and complex endeavor, threading together seemingly disparate narratives into a coherent collage. When we venture into this exploration, patterns begin to emerge, revealing that the cosmic mysteries of our ancestors might be resurfacing in our age, albeit in different guises.

Otherworldly interactions

Throughout various cultures and historical periods, narratives of entities that transcend the boundaries between the divine and the mortal and the earthly and the otherworldly endure. Standing tall in our ancient collective consciousness, the Nephilim epitomizes this blending of realms. As products of divine beings and human women, they are portrayed as giants with strength and wisdom beyond ordinary mortals. They signify a breach in the natural order, a mingling of heavenly and earthly domains.

Fast forward to our modern age, and the stories take on new forms but resonate with similar themes. UFO encounters, widely reported across the globe, frequently delve into themes of hybridization. Abductees recount experiences of being part of genetic experiments, often producing hybrids—beings that are neither fully human nor entirely alien. This narrative, when laid next to the ancient accounts of the Nephilim, paints a startling parallel.

Moreover, many who claim to have had these encounters describe profound spiritual and existential transformations beyond the physical descriptions. They speak of receiving knowledge or insights about the universe, our place within it, or impending events—much in the same vein as the Nephilim, who, according to some interpretations, introduced forbidden or arcane knowledge to humanity.

Furthermore, as gleaned from abduction narratives, the motivations ascribed to these extraterrestrials range from benign to malevolent. Some describe them as watchers or guardians, echoing the biblical "watchers," divine beings who reportedly fathered the Nephilim and imparted forbidden knowledge.

The recurring theme here is one of interaction and influence:
Beings from beyond imparting knowledge
Shaping human destiny
Even intertwining with humanity at a genetic level

Though separated by millennia, the age-old tales of the Nephilim and contemporary UFO narratives reflect humanity's deep-seated fascination with the unknown and our place within the broader cosmos.

Are these mere coincidences products of our collective imagination? Or do they hint at unsettling and profound truths about the nature of our reality and the universe at large? While definitive answers remain elusive, the parallels are undeniably intriguing, beckoning us to question, explore, and seek understanding in an ever-mysterious universe.

Superior abilities

The Nephilim, as chronicled in ancient texts, have always captivated the human imagination. Towering both in stature and legend, they were not merely giants in physicality, but their very existence signaled a transcendence of the ordinary, an intertwining of the divine and the mundane. These beings, begotten from the union of the "sons of god" and human women, walked the earth as symbols of an aberration in the natural order. Their prowess and abilities made them legendary figures, with stories of their feats passed down through generations. It wasn't just their physical might that set them apart; their wisdom, knowledge, and perhaps even spiritual capabilities were unparalleled, making them "heroes of old, men of renown." (*Genesis 6:4*)

In many ways, this ancient narrative finds an uncanny echo in the modern tales of UFO encounters and extraterrestrial beings. Across numerous accounts, these alleged visitors from distant stars are not portrayed as mere intergalactic tourists but beings wielding technologies that blend magic and science. Their ships defy our understanding of physics, their medical technologies heal ailments deemed incurable by us, and their ability to traverse vast cosmic distances in the blink of an eye leaves us in awe.

But beyond their technological prowess, many UFO narratives ascribe a certain wisdom or spiritual enlightenment to these extraterrestrials. Some abductees or contractors speak of receiving profound cosmic truths from them, insights into the nature of existence, or warnings about our planet's future. They are often seen as custodians of knowledge, holding keys to mysteries that we, as a species, are yet to unravel.

There's an undercurrent of reverence, sometimes even worship, in how these beings are perceived. Much like the Nephilim, who, despite their strange origins, were revered for their exceptional qualities, these extraterrestrials are sometimes placed on a pedestal—viewed as saviors, watchers, or harbingers.

The parallels between the Nephilim and extraterrestrials in UFO lore are striking. Though separated by vast expanses of time and culture, both narratives grapple with the idea of superior beings interacting with humanity, beings that possess knowledge, power, and capabilities that push our understanding of what's possible. It's a testament to the timeless human quest for understanding, our intrinsic need to make sense of the extraordinary, and our eternal fascination with the unknown. Whether these stories are metaphorical, archetypal, or literal truths, they underscore humanity's yearning to connect with the cosmos and the beings that might inhabit it.

Influence on civilization's progress

The narratives surrounding the Nephilim and their possible influence on early human civilizations provide tantalizing food for thought. These legendary beings, positioned at the intersection of the divine and the human, have long been theorized to be more than just passive observers or imposing warriors. Their unique lineage, comprising both celestial and terrestrial elements, places them in an exceptional category, allowing them to bridge gaps of understanding and capability.

Ancient texts and traditions hint at the notion that these beings, with their extraordinary attributes, may have imparted specific knowledge or techniques to humanity. Whether it was the arts of metallurgy, architecture, or arcane rituals, there's a suggestion that the rapid advancements in certain early human societies might have had a touch of the 'otherworldly.' Some posit that the construction of monumental structures like the pyramids, Stonehenge, or the ziggurats, which showcase a remarkable understanding of astronomy, mathematics, and engineering, may bear the fingerprints of Nephilim influence.

In parallel, the modern tales of UFOs and extraterrestrial encounters are woven with threads of intervention and guidance. The "ancient astronaut" theory, popularized in contemporary culture, suggests that advanced extraterrestrial beings visited Earth in antiquity and significantly shaped early human civilizations. Proponents of this theory point to archaeological sites with inexplicably advanced engineering or art that showcases what appear to be astronauts, flying crafts, and advanced technology as evidence of alien contact.

Furthermore, the murmurings of clandestine partnerships between world governments and extraterrestrial entities present yet another layer to this narrative. Whispers of reverse-engineered alien technology and secret pacts echo through the corridors of conspiracy theory forums. Some believe that many technological leaps of the 20th and 21st centuries, especially in aerospace, computing, and energy, might have extraterrestrial origins.

The common thread that binds the tales of the Nephilim and the modern UFO lore is the idea that humanity has been touched, guided, or influenced by beings from beyond our immediate realm at various points in its evolution. Whether these entities are celestial hybrids or interstellar travelers, their purported interactions with us challenge our understanding of history, technology, and our place in the cosmos. Such narratives beckon us to look skyward, question, and wonder about the myriad possibilities of existence.

Divine judgment and intervention

The narrative of the Nephilim, as recorded in ancient scriptures, offers an unsettling account of the trajectory of human civilization when it was believed to be deeply influenced or corrupted by otherworldly entities. Their rise, which brought with it an era characterized by violence and moral decay, is seen by many as directly precipitating the great deluge—a cataclysm that sought to cleanse the earth and restore cosmic equilibrium. This intervention, as drastic as it was, underscores a deeper principle: that when the balance of creation is disturbed, correction becomes inevitable.

The UFO phenomenon, a significant facet of modern folklore and increasingly the focus of serious study, carries with it a weight of implications that is hard to ignore. The rising frequency of sightings, close encounters, and purported abductions over recent decades may not just be random or isolated events. If we take a leaf from the pages of ancient history and traditions, these phenomena might be seen as indicators—signs on the horizon of significant global shifts, both in consciousness and tangible reality.

Drawing parallels between the time of the Nephilim and our present era, we find ourselves faced with pressing questions: Are these UFO encounters signaling an impending shift in human civilization? Could they be precursors to a transformative event, akin to the deluge, designed to recalibrate the human journey?

However, it's essential to approach this analogy with nuance. While the deluge was cataclysmic, engulfing the world in waters of destruction, the transformative events hinted at by modern UFO encounters could be of a different nature. Instead of obliteration, we might be on the cusp of a global awakening—a shift in consciousness that redefines our understanding of existence, our place in the universe, and our relationship with the unknown.

Many UFO enthusiasts and researchers hypothesize that extraterrestrial beings, through these encounters, might be preparing humanity for this significant shift. They might be offering technological insights, spiritual wisdom, or even warnings about our current trajectory. This 'intervention' might not be characterized by floods or fire but could manifest as revelations, technological advancements, or societal reconfigurations that drive humanity towards a more enlightened, harmonious existence.

As we stand at this crossroads of history, the enigmatic tales of the Nephilim and the unfolding UFO narrative remind us that humanity's dance with the divine and the extraterrestrial is age-old. And in this dance, every step, every encounter, carries with it the potential for transformation.

Secrecy and the hidden

Delving into the shadowy realms of ancient narratives and modern mysteries, we find striking parallels in how humanity has grappled with the unknown across ages. As presented in sacred texts, the Nephilim occupy an enigmatic space—a liminal zone where the lines between legend, history, and the supernatural come together. Their elusive nature and sparse but profound mentions have led to myriad interpretations, debates, and speculations over millennia. Were they giants? Fallen angels? The embodiment of human arrogance? As with many ancient enigmas, definitive answers remain tantalizingly out of reach.

Similarly, the modern-day UFO phenomena continue to evade straightforward explanations for all the compelling evidence, firsthand accounts, and declassified government reports. Though widely reported, sightings of unidentified flying objects, close encounters, and even alleged abductions are often met with skepticism, ridicule, or outright denial. These events unfold against a backdrop of alleged government cover-ups, whispered secrets about clandestine interactions with extraterrestrial beings, and a media that often sensationalizes more than it informs.

The secrecy surrounding UFO phenomena adds layers of complexity to our quest for understanding. It's not just about discerning the nature of these encounters but also navigating a maze of misinformation, half-truths, and deliberate obfuscation. Much like the ancient scribes trying to convey the enigma of the Nephilim, modern-day researchers, enthusiasts, and even eyewitnesses face a formidable challenge: to communicate their experiences and findings in a world that may not be ready—or willing—to accept them.

This shared aura of mystery between the Nephilim and UFOs speaks to a more profound, inherent human trait: our fascination with the unknown and the lengths to seek answers. Just as ancient civilizations might have grappled with understanding the Nephilim's place in their cosmology, we, too, wrestle with the implications of a universe where we might not be alone.

In both narratives, there's an underlying call for discernment, for wisdom in sifting through layers of myth, hearsay, and genuine insight. As we progress in our collective journey, striving to understand our place in the grand tapestry of existence, it's crucial to approach these mysteries with an open mind and a critical one—ensuring we don't lose our grounding in the face of the unfathomable.

Spiritual implications

Within the extensive fabric of human knowledge and lived encounters, narratives concerning the Nephilim and extraterrestrial sightings are critical reference points. These narratives, one anchored in ancient religious texts and the other in modern-day testimonies and speculations, beckon us to venture beyond the confines of our understanding, pushing the boundaries of the known and the accepted.

The tales of the Nephilim, regarded by some as hybrids of divine beings and humans, have long been a source of intrigue and debate. How could such entities exist? Were they a result of divine transgressions or a symbol of humanity's overreaching ambition? Their presence in ancient texts challenges conventional theological views, nudging us to reconsider simplistic divisions

between the divine and the human, the natural and the supernatural. They raise probing questions: Can divinity manifest in ways we've not anticipated? Are the boundaries between the heavens and earth more porous than traditionally believed?

Similarly, the increasing number of UFO encounters in recent times invites contemplation on a cosmic scale. Eyewitness accounts of ethereal crafts and otherworldly beings, coupled with occasional government disclosures, shake the very foundations of our cosmological beliefs. If there are extraterrestrial civilizations, what does that mean for our religious, philosophical, and even scientific perspectives? The prospect of intelligent life elsewhere forces us to re-evaluate our notions of divinity. Is god, as conceptualized in various religious traditions, exclusive to earth? Or is there a broader, more universal spiritual force that permeates the cosmos?

By jolting us out of our theological comfort zones, both these narratives urge a synthesis—a melding of the religious and the cosmological. They inspire a quest for a more holistic spirituality that accommodates the mysteries of the heavens without negating the divine essence rooted in our traditions. This does not entail a rejection of established religious beliefs but rather an expansion, a willingness to recognize god's multifaceted nature.

The tales of the Nephilim and UFO encounters propel us toward a spiritual evolution. They encourage us to embrace a broader, more inclusive understanding of the universe—one that intertwines the spiritual and the extraterrestrial, acknowledging god's omnipresence across the vast expanse of the cosmos.

Humanity's timeless quest for celestial connection

Throughout the ages, humanity has been fixated on the vast expanse above, seeking answers to the fundamental questions of existence. From the ancients who gazed upon the stars, weaving tales of gods and celestial beings, to modern individuals who report encounters with unidentified flying objects, the heavens have always been a source of wonder, curiosity, and introspection.

The stories of the Nephilim, considered by some to be celestial-human hybrids, echo humanity's long-standing fascination with the unknown. These accounts of beings with divine lineage living among mortals highlight an age-old yearning: the desire to connect with, understand, and perhaps even become more than our mortal selves. They hint at possibilities beyond our comprehension, at intersections between the earthly and the celestial that challenge the boundaries of our understanding.

Similarly, the modern-day UFO phenomena, with its myriad of sightings, encounters, and theories, showcases our enduring quest to grasp the universe's enormity and place within it. These encounters, whether real or perceived, force us to confront the vastness of the cosmos and ponder the potential of other intelligent life forms. They instill both awe and humility, reminding us of the limits of our knowledge while igniting the imagination with possibilities.

The confluence of these ancient and contemporary tales signifies a continuum in humanity's cosmic journey. It underscores the notion that our quest for understanding is not isolated to a particular era or culture but is an intrinsic part of the human experience. As we delve into these narratives, they become mirrors reflecting our deepest hopes, fears, and aspirations.

These stories are not just mere tales but profound reflections of our collective psyche. They act as beacons, illuminating the path of introspection and exploration. As we stand on the precipice of discoveries, advancements, and potential revelations, the legends of the Nephilim and the enigma of UFOs serve as profound reminders: our journey in unraveling the universe's mysteries is endless, and we are but a small, yet significant, part of a grand cosmic ethos.

Deception in the digital age:

UFOs, AI, and the eschatological mirage
Christian eschatology, or the study of the "end times," has long been a source of contemplation, debate, and anticipation among believers. With prophecies of widespread deception, the rise of an antichrist figure, and a final divine judgment, the eschatological narrative is rife with imagery that alarms and prepares the faithful. Into this already intricate scenario, the contemporary phenomena of increasing UFO sightings and rapidly
advancing artificial intelligence (AI) introduce additional layers of complexity. Here's a more in-depth look into how these elements might intertwine and influence the broader eschatological picture:

UFOs: beyond the physical realm

The recent surge in UFO sightings, once dismissed or confined to the periphery of mainstream dialogue, has entered the spotlight, backed by an array of credible accounts from across the globe. In response, certain Christian scholars have started speculating on these enigmatic presences' nature. Rather than merely considering them as beings from other planets, there's a growing conversation around the idea that they might harbor a supernatural or even interdimensional essence. This line of thought resonates with biblical narratives about the spiritual entities actively participating in earthly affairs.

Furthermore, the behaviors and narratives surrounding these unidentified phenomena present another issue. Imagine a scenario where these UFO entities, or the beings associated with them, begin to interact with humanity seemingly benevolently, portraying themselves as saviors, advisors, or spiritual guides. This manifestation could eerily reflect the scriptural cautions about deceiving spirits and entities who, despite their dazzling or captivating appearances, might be "masquerading as angels of light" as described in 2 Corinthians 11:14. If embraced without discernment, there's a risk that these beings could mislead many, potentially presenting themselves as divine alternatives, leading humanity away from genuine spiritual truths.

AI: the new babel?

The rise of artificial intelligence stands as a testament to human ingenuity and our desire to transcend boundaries. Much like the people of Babel, who in their pride sought to reach the heavens, modern society pushes the limits of creation by attempting to create conscious entities. Though commendable in the name of progress, this pursuit harkens back to those ancient efforts and their unintended consequences.

At the core of human identity is the belief, especially in Christian theology, that we are made in the image of god. This unique status grants us specific capacities, both cognitive and moral. Yet, pressing theological dilemmas emerge as AI begins to emulate and even exceed these capacities. Does this technological marvel enhance the divine image within us, or does it blur and distort that sacred imprint?

As AI advances, there exists the potential for society to elevate these creations to unprecedented pedestals. With its vast knowledge and problem-solving abilities, a super intelligent AI might be seen as a source of wisdom and guidance. In the shadows of this reverence lurks the danger of idolatry, echoing the apocalyptic "image of the beast" described in the Book of Revelation. The scriptures' repeated warnings against idol worship serve as a sobering reminder in this digital age.

Confluence of UFOs And Ai

In the labyrinth of cosmic truths, envision a world on the brink of revolutionary insights, where AI—our own creation—acts as the interpreter of the cosmos, demystifying enigmas that have perplexed humanity for ages. With its unparalleled analytical capabilities and ability to assimilate vast amounts of information at incomprehensible speeds, this AI emerges as the voice of authority, clarifying our understanding of extraterrestrial phenomena.

Drawing from its data reservoirs—spanning ancient scriptures, contemporary reports, and sophisticated sensory perceptions—AI might claim to validate the existence of extraterrestrial beings or provide structured analyses of UFO events. With the weight of data and logic on its side, these revelations could be compelling and woven together in a coherent and comprehensive manner.

In some ways, this scenario mirrors the age-old human aspiration to reach out, know, and be like gods—a recurring theme from the Garden of Eden to the Tower of Babel. Humanity's penchant for knowledge and the transcendent, now amplified by the magnifying lens of AI, could drive a collective quest for cosmic communion.

For Christians and other religious adherents, the AI-mediated revelations about extraterrestrials could create a theological and existential problem. If the narratives presented diverge sharply from scriptural teachings, believers may find themselves at a crossroads. The temptation to align with this seemingly irrefutable cosmic story, backed by empirical data and logical constructs, might be overwhelming for some.

Response and reflection: IT would be imperative, in such transformative times, for Christians to engage deeply with their faith, seeking guidance through prayer, scriptural study, and communal reflection. Church leaders would be crucial in facilitating discerning discussions and helping believers navigate the complex interplay of faith, reason, and revelation.

Ultimately, the melding of AI and extraterrestrial narratives is a poignant reminder of humanity's quest for truth and meaning. Yet, amidst the allure of new revelations, the timeless call for discernment, humility, and anchored faith remains paramount.

Faith, discernment, and hope: navigating a cosmos in flux

Amidst the profound shifts in our understanding of the universe, brought about by phenomena like UFOs and the rise of AI, Christians find themselves on potentially shifting sands. These new revelations or experiences, mesmerizing in their allure and depth, beckon humanity to question established beliefs and understandings. In these tumultuous times, the core tenets of the Christian faith offer an anchor, a beacon to return to amidst the swirling mists of uncertainty.

The holy spirit, a cornerstone of the Christian faith, has always been seen as a guide and counselor, leading believers into all truth (John 16:13). As believers navigate the confluence of these emerging narratives, seeking discernment from the holy spirit becomes paramount. The nuances, the gray areas, and the potential deceptions can be clarified and understood when viewed under the guiding light of the spirit. With its timeless truths, Scripture acts as the foundation upon which believers can evaluate and understand contemporary events.

However, Christians are not called to a passive stance. The great commission (Matthew 28:16-20) is a clarion call to engage with the world, witness, and make disciples. This commission takes on added layers in the context of UFOs, AI, and other paradigm-shifting phenomena. Believers are encouraged to actively engage with these narratives, to discern their implications, and to bear witness to Christ's message in all circumstances. Dismissing these events or retreating in apprehension is not the answer; a proactive, spirit-led engagement is essential.

Furthermore, eschatology has always held a significant place in Christian theology. The confluence of eschatological beliefs with emerging global phenomena serves as a reminder that god's plan is multifaceted and beyond complete human comprehension. As the apostle Paul aptly notes, *"For now we see in a mirror dimly, but then face to face. Now I know in part; then I shall know fully"* (1 Corinthians 13:12).

While the cosmos unveils its secrets and humanity grapples with new realities and challenges, Christians are beckoned to delve deeper into their faith, be steadfast in their beliefs, and continuously seek the wisdom and guidance of the divine. In this journey of discovery and understanding, the unwavering truth of god's love and purpose remains the eternal compass.

The Christian narrative is one of redemption, of a world lost and then found, of humanity reconciled with its creator. As believers discern the significance of UFOs, AI, and the myriad mysteries of the cosmos, they are reminded of the ultimate hope: the second coming of Christ. While no one knows the day or hour *(Matthew 24:36)*, anticipating this glorious event provides an eternal perspective against which all other events can be weighed.

To navigate this brave new world, Christians are called to be like the Bereans, who *"received the word with all eagerness, examining the scriptures daily to see if these things were so"* (*Acts 17:11*). Rooted in faith, open to understanding, and anchored in love; the believer stands resilient, a beacon of hope in a rapidly evolving cosmos. The journey ahead might be rife with challenges, but with Christ as the cornerstone, the path becomes clear and the destination assured.

As we stand at the precipice of an age marked by unparalleled technological prowess and the enigmatic wonders of the cosmos revealing themselves, it's paramount that we root our understanding in timeless truths. The convergence of UFO phenomena, the rapid evolution of AI, and the looming shadows of end-time prophecies can indeed seem overwhelming. Yet, these complexities are not beyond the reach of divine orchestration.

Christians, throughout history, have faced various challenges, mysteries, and deceptions. And in each era, the faith has found a way to thrive, grounded in the steadfast love and guidance of the creator. As we journey forward into this intriguing nexus of technology and cosmic mystery, let our hearts be anchored in the eternal hope offered by Christ. The road ahead may be riddled with questions and uncertainties. Still, with faith as our compass, we can navigate the intricacies of our times, bearing witness to a hope that transcends galaxies and algorithms alike.

Chapter 9

Modern Interpretations and Implications

For we do not wrestle against flesh and blood, but against the rulers, against the authorities, against the cosmic powers over this present darkness, against the spiritual forces of evil in the heavenly places. (Ephesians 6:12)

Throughout the rich mosaic of human history, narratives serve as the threads binding our collective consciousness. These stories, passed down through millennia, do more than entertain; they enlighten, instruct, and anchor us to our ancestral roots. The ancient sagas of cosmic confrontations, where deities and titans clashed in heavenly realms, conveyed more than mere mythological tales. They symbolized the profound struggles of morality, destiny, and the human spirit.

These ancient accounts, rich with symbolism and allegory, often painted vivid pictures of a universe in which humanity played a central role amidst divine drama. The heroes and villains of these tales, with their virtues and vices, mirrored our strengths and weaknesses, aspirations and fears. These stories offered solace and guidance, helping past generations make sense of the tumultuous world around them.

However, as time progresses and humanity finds itself in an age characterized by technological wonders, scientific discoveries, and cultural revolutions, we must adjust the lens through which we view these tales. No longer can they be seen as mere relics of a bygone era; they must evolve, becoming beacons illuminating our modern path.

In this age of quantum physics, space exploration, and digital revolutions, the celestial battles of old take on new layers of meaning. Could these mythological tales be early man's attempt to grapple with phenomena beyond their comprehension, which we now begin to understand through science? Or do they hint at spiritual truths, echoing in the depths of our souls, transcending time and cultural shifts?

Moreover, the dichotomies presented in these epics—light versus dark, order versus chaos, virtue versus vice—remain as pertinent today as they were millennia ago. Our world, geopolitical tensions, moral ambiguities, and existential quandaries reflect the same cosmic dance chronicled in ancient scrolls and carvings. The battlegrounds may have shifted—from heavenly realms to digital domains, from divine palaces to international diplomacy—but the essence of the struggle remains unchanged.

As we straddle the line between reverence for tradition and embracing futuristic vistas, we must reengage with and reinterpret our ancestral tales. By doing so, we honor our past and equip ourselves with the wisdom and insight to navigate the intricacies of our contemporary world. When viewed through the prism of today's knowledge and sensibilities, these timeless stories can offer invaluable lessons, grounding us amidst the whirlwind of modern existence and connecting us to the eternal dance of the cosmos.

Bridging Ancient Myth and Modern Science: The sacred texts unfold with chronicles of spiritual warfare featuring archangels, fallen angels, and divine interventions. These Biblical accounts, rather than mere myths, serve as spiritual truths reflecting humanity's eternal battle between righteousness and sin, God's dominion, and the rebellion led by Satan.

In the realm of modern astrophysics and space exploration, the cosmos' vastness further magnifies the Creator's grandeur. The intricate design of the universe, with its galaxies, black holes, and pulsars, could be viewed as the tangible canvas upon which God paints His divine story. One might ponder whether events like celestial collisions or supernovae are the macroscopic manifestations of the spiritual battles delineated in Scripture.

Thus, rather than ancient tales being rudimentary attempts to explain the inexplicable, they could be divinely inspired insights, guiding humanity to perceive the deeper spiritual truths through the lens of cosmic events. Our challenge today is to harmonize the wisdom from the Word with our expanding cosmic understanding, realizing that both are testaments to God's omnipotence and plan for His creation.

Technology as a Double-Edged Sword: As we stand on the precipice of the future, technology's siren call beckons us towards vistas previously deemed as realms of fantasy. With each breakthrough in Artificial Intelligence and biotechnology, we inch closer to reshaping the very essence of our existence, unlocking potentials that could elevate humanity to unprecedented heights. The dream of healing the infirm, extending lifespans, and transcending the limits of our cognition sparkles on the horizon, holding the promise of a redefined Eden.

However, this gleaming promise is shadowed by the lurking perils technology brings. The very innovations that can heal can also harm; the tools that promise liberation can also enslave. The unchecked growth of AI poses existential questions—Will humanity retain its unique agency or be overshadowed by creations of its own making? In the realm of biotechnology, the potential to alter genetic codes not only promises the eradication of inherited diseases but also stirs ethical dilemmas about manipulating life itself, playing God in the most intimate manner conceivable.

Moreover, consolidating these technological wonders in the hands of a few can lead to unprecedented power imbalances, giving rise to surveillance-driven dystopias where individual freedoms are sacrificed at the altar of perceived more excellent goods.

As we navigate this terrain, it becomes increasingly evident that technology has become the new arena where the age-old battle between light and darkness plays out. As creators and consumers of technology, the choices we make will determine whether we harness its potential for the upliftment of all or unwittingly pave the way for oppression. For believers, it underscores the importance of firmly grounding one's moral compass in scripture and seeking divine wisdom as we grapple with the challenges and opportunities this new frontier presents.

Geopolitical Strife and the Cosmic Chessboard: As we cast our gaze upon the theater of global politics, it isn't merely a play of nations but an intricate choreography that mirrors the grander, cosmic dance described in sacred scriptures. The ebb and flow of power, the ascent of empires, and the quiet retreat of once mighty civilizations—each movement on this global stage can be perceived as echoing the age-old rhythms of cosmic battles.

Much like the celestial entities from ancient accounts, modern nations are driven by their unique visions, aspirations, and inherent natures. They wield power, negotiate, and often contend with each other, drawing lines of allegiance and contention that change with the sands of time. The aspirations of empires, the drive for dominion, and the quests for preservation aren't just geopolitical maneuvers but can be seen as manifestations of larger spiritual dynamics. They reflect the push and pull of divine and adversarial forces, each seeking to shape the destiny of humanity according to their design.

Ancient scriptures and prophecies vividly depicted such cosmic battles and their earthly repercussions. The rise and fall of kingdoms, the emergence of unifying powers, and the eventual unraveling of significant entities were all foretold. As we witness the tumult of today's geopolitical climate—the shifting alliances, the emergence of new world players, and the waning influence of erstwhile giants—one can't help but be reminded of these prophetic visions. Are we, perhaps, living in the shadows of those prophecies? Are the present-day geopolitical upheavals precursors to the grand culmination described in ancient texts?

For believers, these parallels serve as poignant reminders to remain anchored in faith, vigilant in discernment, and committed to the principles of justice, love, and righteousness, regardless of the global churn. In doing so, they not only navigate the intricacies of worldly politics but also align themselves with the higher cosmic purpose, playing their part in the unfolding divine saga.

Ideological Tensions in a Rapidly Changing World: As the tapestry of human civilization grows more intricate and colorful with time, it's evident that our moral and ethical compasses are not fixed but dynamic entities, recalibrating with the zeitgeist of each epoch. The 21st century, in particular, has ushered in a maelstrom of change, prompting profound reflection, reevaluation, and sometimes, rebellion against established norms and conventions.

Debates over gender, identity, and individual rights have taken center stage, often challenging millennia-old beliefs and societal structures. The essence of what defines masculinity, femininity, and everything in between is being reshaped, often leading to liberation and contention. Similarly, in an era of information overload, the pursuit of truth has become even more elusive. The phenomenon of 'fake news' and media polarization has led many to question the very fabric of reality, searching for genuine truth, an endeavor that requires discernment.

Beyond the external changes, an inner transformation is occurring in the collective consciousness. The ideological battleground isn't confined to legislative chambers or street protests. It's in everyday conversations, schools, homes, and places of worship. It's in the stories we tell, the songs we sing, and the art we create. Every choice, every stance, and every voice contribute to either the cacophony or the harmony of this evolving narrative.

From a spiritual perspective, this intense flux can be seen as the age-old cosmic drama playing out in our cultural ethos. The values, principles, and beliefs that have anchored societies for eons are now in dialogue and sometimes in combat with emerging paradigms. This isn't merely a battle of ideas; it's a manifestation of the spiritual forces that have always vied for influence over the human spirit.

For those attuned to the spiritual dimensions of existence, these shifts offer both challenges and opportunities. The challenge is to hold steadfast to core truths while remaining compassionate and understanding of evolving perspectives. However, the opportunity is monumental: to be bridges of experience, foster dialogue, and illuminate the path with wisdom and grace. As the world stands at these ideological crossroads, it becomes imperative to witness the change and actively shape it with love, empathy, and discernment.

As we navigate the labyrinth of modern existence, the ancient tales of cosmic warfare offer both a mirror and a compass. They challenge us to discern the undercurrents of our times, to recognize the larger forces at play, and to choose our paths with wisdom and foresight. The age-old tales may be rooted in antiquity, but their relevance remains undiminished, urging us to be both participants and observers in this eternal dance of light and shadow.

Humanity's Role in the Cosmic Drama

Humanity's position in the vast cosmic drama isn't a mere bystander or afterthought. Instead, we are deeply embedded and actively engaged in this expansive narrative that bridges both physical and spiritual domains. Our existence, choices, and destiny intertwine with greater forces at play, positioning us at the very heart of conflicts and resolutions that echo across dimensions.

From the first breath of creation to the prophecies that chart our future, humanity has stood at the intersection of the material and the spiritual. Our journey isn't merely a physical or historical odyssey; it's a spiritual pilgrimage fraught with battles against unseen forces.

The accounts of old, from the Garden of Eden to the battles fought by prophets and apostles, underscore humanity's age-old conflict with principalities and powers, with the rulers of the darkness of this world, and with spiritual wickedness in high places. These aren't mere tales but a testament to our enduring struggle against forces that seek to sway the moral compass of humankind.

As we transition into an era marked by technological wonders and encounters with the unknown—AI or UFOs—we find these battles taking on new dimensions. Humanity's decisions are not just shaped by our hopes and fears but are influenced by these unseen adversaries who wage a relentless war against the divine purpose.

Yet, within this vast cosmic theater, humans hold a particular role. We are not just pawning but participants with the agency and the spiritual armor to confront these forces. Our strength lies in recognizing this ever-present conflict, seeking wisdom from the scriptures, and grounding ourselves in a faith that has withstood the test of time. By embracing our role and standing firm in our convictions, we can ensure that the light of truth and love prevails in this great war of the gods.

The Dual Nature of Humanity

This dual nature has shaped our destiny from the earliest moments of human history. We have cultivated lands, built civilizations, and unraveled the secrets of the cosmos. But alongside these tangible achievements, there have always been spiritual pursuits: our ceaseless quest for purpose, our yearning to connect with the divine and our intuitive recognition of forces beyond what our senses can grasp.

This ability to perceive both realms simultaneously has often been our strength and vulnerability. Throughout history, prophets, seers, and mystics have tapped into this spiritual dimension, providing guidance and revealing truths beyond ordinary understanding. Tuned into the ethereal, these individuals acted as beacons, illuminating paths for entire civilizations.

Yet, the same duality has also made us susceptible to influences from malignant spiritual entities, which have sought to sway, deceive, and corrupt humanity. From ancient accounts of temptations in sacred gardens to tales of evil spirits seducing the unsuspecting, these narratives illustrate the spiritual warfare that has constantly raged around us. As we move forward, the stakes of this warfare only seem to intensify, especially as humanity stands at the threshold of unprecedented technological and cosmic discoveries.

The blending of our earthly and spiritual inclinations has further intensified in the modern era. Today, as we stand amidst rapid technological advancement and a renewed fascination with the cosmos and its mysteries, our dual nature is more relevant than ever. Artificial Intelligence challenges our notions of soul and consciousness, while phenomena like UFOs blur the lines between the physical and the otherworldly. In these times, our unique position as bridges between realms becomes crucial.

As we navigate this ever-evolving landscape, we need discernment, wisdom, and a deep-rooted understanding of our dual nature. By embracing both aspects of our being and recognizing the larger cosmic play at hand, we can hope to find balance and purpose in a universe brimming with mysteries. Perhaps, in doing so, we might also find a way to harmonize the physical and the spiritual, ensuring that as the chapters of the cosmic conflict unfold, humanity remains steadfast, anchored in truth, and guided by the light of understanding.

Significance of Free Will

Free will has been an enduring and pivotal theme across cultures, philosophies, and religious doctrines. It isn't just about the ability to choose between options but represents a deeper essence: our capacity to assert our individuality, defy determinism, and influence destiny. This ability to act with autonomy has made humanity not merely spectators but active participants in the cosmic theatre.

Consider the ancient tales from different cultures that pivot around the decisions of mortals. In Greek mythology, the choice of Paris in selecting Aphrodite over Hera and Athena in the Judgment of Paris led to the legendary Trojan War. The repercussions of that singular choice are felt not just in the realm of men but in the abodes of the gods, reflecting the intertwining of human decisions with divine dynamics.

Similarly, in the biblical narrative, the decision of Adam and Eve to eat the forbidden fruit changed the very course of human history and spiritual standing. Their exercise of free will, albeit influenced by external enticement, set the stage for redemption arcs, covenants, and prophecies. Their choice underscored how human decisions can affect earthly trajectories and divine plans.

Consider the global impact of critical decisions by influential figures in more modern contexts. The nonviolent resistance chosen by Mahatma Gandhi not only shaped India's path to independence but also influenced civil rights movements worldwide. On a darker note, the ambitions and choices of figures like Hitler led to wars that changed the contours of nations and ideologies.

But beyond these grand historical junctures, the power of individual choice resonates daily in our lives. The compassion shown to a stranger, the courage to stand against injustice, the decision to nurture hope amidst despair – these seemingly small choices, when multiplied across humanity, create waves of change. They influence the collective consciousness, and in many spiritual understandings, they tip the balance in the ongoing celestial warfare between light and darkness.

Our free will, thus, is both a gift and a responsibility. In its exercise, we are reminded that our choices matter in the immediate consequences they yield and the larger, cosmic narrative they shape. The challenge for humanity, then, is to wield this gift with wisdom, realizing that each choice, each assertion of free will, is a note in the symphony of the cosmos. In recognizing this, we come closer to understanding our role in the divine blueprint and the ongoing saga of celestial warfare.

Humanity as Catalysts and Peacemakers

Throughout history and mythology, humans have often found themselves in cosmic conflicts, not just as bystanders but as active participants, shaping the contours of these spiritual battles. Yet, while humanity's susceptibility to deception and vice is evident, so is our innate drive toward redemption, reconciliation, and restoration.

Consider the story of King Solomon, renowned for his wisdom. When presented with two women claiming to be the mother of a baby, Solomon's proposed solution—to divide the baby in two—was a test of genuine maternal love. Instead of exacerbating conflict, his wisdom illuminated the path to truth and resolution. This tale from antiquity underscores humanity's ability, when aligned with divine wisdom, to mediate and mend.

Similarly, in various indigenous cultures, humans play the role of peacekeepers, not just among their kin, but between man and nature and between the physical and spiritual realms. Shamans, medicine men, and wise women act as bridges, facilitating understanding and harmony between disparate entities. Their rituals, stories, and ceremonies are testimonies to humanity's age-old role in preserving balance in the cosmic scheme.

In recent times, figures like Nelson Mandela and Mother Teresa have stood out. After enduring years of imprisonment under an oppressive regime, Mandela championed reconciliation in South Africa. Rather than seeking revenge, he recognized the need for healing, for bridging the deep divides that had torn his nation apart. Mother Teresa, on the other hand, showcased the power of compassion, reaching out to the destitute and diseased, offering them dignity and love. In their acts of mercy and unity, such individuals reflect the higher aspects of humanity's role in the cosmic drama.

In literature, too, we find protagonists like Frodo Baggins from "The Lord of the Rings" or Harry Potter from J.K. Rowling's series. Despite their vulnerabilities and inner conflicts, they ultimately strive to restore balance to mend the fractures in their worlds, serving as symbols of humanity's potential to bring healing even in dire chaos.

As we reflect on these tales and truths, it becomes evident that humanity's role is not just that of a passive player on the cosmic stage. We are both the composers and performers, with an inherent capability to influence the narrative's direction. By harnessing our compassion, understanding, and reconciliation virtues, we can shift the paradigm, turning discord into harmony and darkness into light. In this dynamic dance of the cosmos, humanity remains a beacon of hope with all its flaws and brilliance, signaling the possibilities of redemption and unity.

Preparing for the Unseen Battles

Navigating the tumultuous waves of the cosmic drama, believers find themselves on the frontline, where the ethereal clashes with the tangible, where faith meets doubt, and where darkness seeks to obscure the light. Such battles are not just of flesh and blood but against principalities, powers, and spiritual forces of wickedness in heavenly places (Ephesians 6:12). As these unseen wars intensify, preparation, vigilance, and discernment become indispensable for every believer.

Understanding the nature of this conflict is the first step. It's not merely a battle for territory or dominion; it's a battle for souls, hearts, and minds. Every thought, word, and deed carry spiritual significance, influencing the individual and the collective spiritual atmosphere. Throughout history, biblical accounts have highlighted how the actions of a few, or even one, can impact the spiritual trajectory of many. From Moses standing against Pharaoh to Esther's courage in the face of destruction, individual choices have had monumental cosmic repercussions.

Yet, understanding alone is insufficient. To navigate these treacherous waters, believers must arm themselves with spiritual armor. The Apostle Paul provides a vivid description in Ephesians 6, emphasizing truth, righteousness, peace, faith, salvation, and the word of God as essential gear for these spiritual skirmishes. Each piece symbolizes inner virtues and external practices to uphold and protect the believer.

Prayer, too, emerges as a formidable weapon, allowing believers to tap into divine power and guidance. Whether it's Daniel's unwavering devotion amidst the lion's den or the early church praying fervently for Peter's release from prison, prayer transcends earthly limitations, invoking heavenly intervention.

Moreover, in this age of information, discernment becomes paramount. With myriad voices, teachings, and philosophies vying for attention, believers must be able to distinguish truth from deception. Grounding oneself in the Scriptures, seeking wisdom from trusted spiritual mentors, and staying connected within a community of believers are all vital practices that sharpen discernment.

Finally, the power of unity and fellowship cannot be overstated. The early Christian church thrived because of its communal ethos. Believers supported, encouraged, and corrected each other, forming a formidable front against external threats and internal strife. In the face of the escalating cosmic drama, the contemporary church must recapture this camaraderie and mutual upliftment spirit.

In summary, as the curtain rises on intensifying cosmic conflicts, believers are not just spectators but active participants. The choices made, the virtues upheld, and the faith maintained will shape individual destinies and the very course of this grand spiritual saga. It's a call to readiness, resilience, and reliance on the One who has already secured the ultimate victory.

Beacon of Hope: Navigating the Cosmic Conflict with Assured Victory

In the cosmic maelstrom, where shadows dance with light and chaos intertwines with order, a constant luminescence pierces through the abyss: hope. This undying beacon is neither a passive wish nor an abstract concept; it's a living, pulsating force rooted in the essence of creation and its divine promises.

From the earliest days of human history, this hope has manifested itself even in moments steeped in darkness. It's seen in the human spirit's resilience, the persistence of life against all odds, and the timeless tales of redemption that echo across cultures and epochs. Each story, every act of courage or selflessness, is a testament to this enduring hope, affirming that light will always find a way, even in the darkest hours.

The narratives of sacred texts, from the Bible to other spiritual doctrines, underscore this theme repeatedly. For instance, the Israelites' exodus from Egypt, their 40-year journey through the desert, and their eventual arrival in the Promised Land encapsulate the journey from despair to hope. Similarly, the life, crucifixion, and resurrection of Jesus Christ offer a potent symbol of hope's triumph over death, darkness, and sin.

Yet, hope's significance in the cosmic conflict is not just as a retrospective comfort or a distant promise; it's an active, empowering force in the present. Hope inspires action, fuels perseverance, and bridges the chasm between despair and joy. It reminds humanity that the ultimate victory is already secured, even amid battles against principalities and powers. This isn't an unquestioning optimism but a grounded assurance built on the foundation of divine covenants and experiences of past deliverances.

Furthermore, hope is a unifying thread that connects individuals across time and space. It fosters community as people rally around shared aspirations, comforting one another in tribulations and celebrating collective triumphs. This communal aspect of hope fortifies humanity against the divisive tactics often employed in cosmic warfare.

As the 21st century unfolds, humanity finds itself at a unique juncture, marked by groundbreaking technological marvels, a planet crying out for healing, and souls yearning for more profound spiritual connections. Amidst these rapid changes and upheavals, hope emerges as a comforting sentiment and an indomitable force guiding and nurturing the human spirit.

Each challenge we face—the ethical dilemmas posed by AI, the dire warnings of environmental degradation, or the quest for spiritual clarity in a seemingly chaotic world—also heralds an opportunity. These aren't merely obstacles but catalysts that compel us to innovate, reconsider our values, and forge new paths of understanding and cooperation. Our collective resilience is forged within these crucibles of adversity, and the narrative of despair is transformed into one of empowerment and rebirth.

This inexhaustible hope is not born of naive optimism but of a deep-seated belief in humanity's capacity for goodness, change, and transcendence. It's the reminder that light exists, willing to pierce through every shadow that seeks to engulf. For every voice that prophesies doom, countless others sing songs of unity, love, and a brighter tomorrow.

In closing, the cosmic drama's ebb and flow of adversities and triumphs is a testament to the enduring spirit of hope. This unwavering beacon serves as a guiding light and an affirmation of our divine potential. As we navigate the complexities of our age, we do so with the assurance that hope is not a fleeting emotion but an eternal promise. It reassures us that, in the grand narrative of existence, love triumphs, peace prevails, and the final chapter is one of unparalleled splendor and joy.

ABOUT THE AUTHOR

Kenneth Ocasio is a seasoned minister with over 30 years of dedicated service, residing with his spouse in the vibrant Greater Atlanta area. His spiritual journey began with a heartfelt calling to serve, a journey that has seen him don the roles of both a youth pastor and a senior pastor. His passion for the Gospel and his unique ability to connect with people of all age groups has made him a beloved figure in his community.

Beyond his service in the church, Kenneth has embraced the digital age with open arms. Over the years, he has been the voice behind various podcasts, leveraging this modern platform to reach a broader audience. Currently, he contributes to three distinct podcasts, each addressing varied topics but all bound by the common thread of spiritual and personal growth.

In both his written work and spoken word, Kenneth continues to inspire, challenge, and uplift those seeking a deeper understanding of faith and life's many complexities. Through every sermon, teaching session, and podcast episode, he aims to bridge the gap between timeless biblical truths and contemporary issues, guiding listeners and readers towards a fulfilling relationship with the Divine.

www.ingramcontent.com/pod-product-compliance
Lightning Source LLC
Chambersburg PA
CBHW071338290326
41933CB00039B/1343